THE QUILTED SAFARI

by
Donna Wilder

THE QUILTED SAFARI

Table of Contents

Introduction 3
Materials List 4
General Instructions 4
Zebra 7
Lion 8
Giraffe 9
Fish 10
Kangaroo 11
Turtle 12
Cat 12
Elephants 13
Sheep and Ducks 14
Woodland Animals 15
Panda 16
Parrot 17
Safari Wallhanging 18
Count the Animals Wallhanging 19
Turtle and Fish Pillow 21
Girl's Quilted Cat Jacket 23
Templates 26-40

©1997. Donna Wilder. No portion of this book may be reproduced in any form (except where it is indicated for the paper piecing blocks) without written permission of the author. She may be contacted through the publisher.

Published by: FPC Media, P. O. Box 1130, Danbury, CT 06813.

Managing Editor: Patty Bailey
Technical Editor: Carter Houck
Cover Design: Mary Beth Clarke
Type and Graphics: Mimi and John Shimp, SPPS, Inc.
Photography: Brad Stanton Photography

ISBN 0-9655270-2-6

We have made every effort to ensure that the instructions in this book are accurate and complete. We cannot, however, be responsible for human error, typographical mistakes or variations in individual work.

Donna on the set of "Sew Creative."

Several of my past books contain instructions for sampler quilts, but this time I wanted to do something quite different than in the past. I chose to work with an animal theme since it was such a fun idea and the blocks would be so adaptable to other projects. There are so many ways that these blocks can be utilized other than just in the quilt, and we have included four projects to get you started. I also wanted to help quilters expand their horizons by exposing them to many different types of construction methods. These blocks feature many techniques including patchwork, appliqué, paper piecing, invisible machine appliqué, freezer paper appliqué, embroidery stitching, reverse appliqué, etc.

To bring our menagerie to life I called upon the very talented Marsha Evans Moore who has worked with me on several of the "Sew Creative" quilts. Marsha used the wonderful fabrics from the "Nature's Symphony" line from Springs to create the blocks which became our "Quilted Safari" quilt. In addition, to show the versatility of these patterns, Marsha designed four additional pieces based on several of these blocks. These basic blocks could also be used as the foundation for a variety of projects, the only limit is your imagination!

I would like to thank Springs Industries for generously providing the fabric used in the "Quilted Safari" quilt and accessory pieces. In addition I would also like to thank the following companies for their support of my public television series, "Sew Creative" which featured this quilt in its 1000 series: The DMC Corporation, New Home/Janome Sewing Machine Company, June Tailor, Quilter's Newsletter Magazine, Springs Industries, Sulky of America, and Wrights. A big thank you also goes to my friend, Carter Houck, who checked our book for technical accuracy.

In addition, I would like to thank all of the loyal viewers of "Sew Creative". I will continue to bring you crafting and quilting projects, hints and tips, and guests from the best companies in the industry. I hope you will continue to enjoy all of the items we present to you and will watch "Sew Creative" for many years to come.

P.S. If "Sew Creative" is not available in your area, please call your local public television station and request that they run it. It is available at no charge to them and we will be happy to send stations information upon request. Please tell them to direct their requests to: Sew Creative, PO Box 2254, Danbury, CT 06813.

Donna Wild

Materials Needed

45" WIDE COTTON FABRICS IN THE FOLLOWING COLORS:

¼ yard blue floral print
¼ yard beige print
⅜ yard blue streaked print
⅛ yard tan print
¼ yard blue leaf print
¼ yard gold print
⅜ yard gold floral print
¼ yard purple print
⅜ yard magenta print
⅜ yard aqua print
¼ yard dark green print
¼ yard olive green print
¼ yard or 12" x 6" piece tan geometric print
⅜ yard lavender print
¼ yard black
¼ yard white
⅛ yard gold
⅛ yard olive green
⅛ yard tan
¼ yard gray
⅛ yard rust

⅛ yard light brown
⅛ yard medium brown
⅛ yard or 3" x 9" piece off-white
1 yard olive green for binding
1¾ yards dark brown print for sashing
2⅛ yards brown and tan print for borders
2¾ yards 72" wide fabric or 4½ yards 45" fabric for backing
1 twin size Poly-fil® Traditional® quilt batting
Small amount of Poly-fil® polyester fiberfill

ADDITIONAL NOTIONS:

Thread to match fabrics
Six strand embroidery floss – black, white, gold, green, olive, tan, brown and gray
Buttons – two ½" diameter black, two ½" diameter dark brown, two ¼" diameter brown
Invisible nylon thread
½ yard paper backed fusible webbing
Template plastic
Freezer paper

General Instructions

CHOOSING THE FABRIC

Most quilters prefer to work with 100% cotton fabric. There is less distortion with cotton which means smaller pieces fit together more easily. Because of the need to press frequently when piecing, cotton is the best choice since it irons flat. When quilting by hand, your needle will move through cotton fabric with ease.

It is a good idea to check your fabric for colorfastness by washing it in warm water before you begin your quilt. Fabric which continues to bleed after washing should not be used. Washing the fabric will also insure that it is totally preshrunk.

SUPPLIES

In addition to the materials listed above, you will need other tools to complete your quilt:

SHARP SCISSORS – used for fabric cutting only.

SCISSORS, SINGLE EDGE RAZOR, OR CRAFT KNIFE – used to cut the template material.

ROTARY CUTTER, ACRYLIC RULER AND MAT – used when cutting strips, squares and rectangles for strip piecing.

QUILTING THREAD – is stronger than standard sewing thread and is used for hand quilting.

INVISIBLE NYLON THREAD – is used as the top thread when machine quilting.

NEEDLES – in size 14 for machine piecing; size 7-8 for hand piecing; for embroidery use size 7 or 8 sharp or embroidery needles.

STRAIGHT PINS

MARKING PEN OR PENCIL – to mark the quilting designs onto your fabric. Test any marking pen to be sure that it will not run when wet and can be washed out or otherwise erased. A #2 lead pencil may also be used.

IRONING BOARD AND IRON – for pressing your seams as you piece. A steam iron is preferable, but some quilters prefer a dry iron with a damp cloth.

SAFETY PINS – in size #1 or #2 are used to baste your quilt before quilting, unless you thread baste. Place pins no more than 4" to 6" apart, and avoid seams and other areas where you will be stitching.

TEMPLATES

Templates for the pattern pieces are found on pages 26-40. The templates DO NOT INCLUDE SEAM ALLOWANCES. Trace template patterns carefully onto the template plastic. Be sure to include all markings when tracing your templates as these are important for accurate piecing. The templates included are for hand or machine piecing. If you are machine piecing, add ¼" seam allowances to templates BEFORE cutting fabric. Those who hand piece usually mark on seam line and add the seam allowance as they are cutting the fabric pieces.

FINISHING THE QUILT

As you piece the blocks it is important to press seams to one side. Alternate the direction of the sides on pieces that will be joined together. This will eliminate any "bumps" in the seams where they are joined. After piecing the blocks, they *should* measure 12½" square. Yours may be slightly larger or smaller, but as long as they are consistently the same size, don't panic! Trim all blocks to the same size, and as long as the blocks are square, you will be fine.

Press completed blocks with a steam iron to smooth any wrinkles and make them very flat. Do not iron as you would for clothing – a gentle pressing of the iron is what you want. Arrange the blocks as in the photograph on the cover, or in any order that is pleasing to you.

SASHING: Before joining the blocks, you will need to cut sashing strips. Cut 9 strips 2½" x 12½" (or the size of your block). Join these sashing strips to the blocks as shown below.

The length of your quilt should measure approximately 54½". Cut 4 strips 2½" x 54½" (or length of your quilt). Add these strips between the vertical rows of blocks and on each side of the quilt. Cut 2 strips 2½" x 44½" (or width of your quilt) and add to the top and bottom of the quilt top. See below.

BORDERS: *The Quilted Safari* has 6" wide border strips. Cut 2 strips 6½" x 44½" (or the width of your quilt) and join to the the top and bottom of the quilt top. Cut 2 strips 6½" x 70½" (or the length of your quilt) and join to the sides of the quilt top. See Border Figure 1. Arrange remaining tail feathers and attach after border has been added. (See Parrot, page 17 for more details on making tail feathers.)

LAYERING THE QUILT: There are many types of batting available for use in your quilt, both polyester and 100% cotton varieties. Choose the type you like the best. The quilt photographed uses Fairfield Poly-fil® Traditional® batting. It is a good idea to open the batting and let it breathe for a day before you layer your quilt. Cut batting at least 2" larger than the top, all the way around.

Fabric for your backing should be 100% cotton, the same as the quilt top fabric. This should be preshrunk and pressed before layering with the batting and top. Unless you have 72" wide fabric you will need to piece lengths of fabric to fit your quilt, as it is larger than the width of the fabric. Cut the selvages from the backing fabric. Cut the fabric crossgrain into two 2¼ yard pieces and seam together lengthwise. Press seams open flat. Cut the backing fabric at least 2" larger than the quilt top all the way around.

Border Figure 1.

THREAD BASTING THE QUILT: Place backing wrong side up on a flat surface. Place batting on top of the backing, then the quilt top right side up and pin to secure. Baste the three layers together with long stitches starting in the center and working toward the edges. Check to see that grain lines on top and backing remain even as you baste.

PIN BASTING THE QUILT: Use #1 or #2 rust-proof safety pins for pin basting. Lay the backing wrong side up on a flat surface, then the batting, then the quilt top, right side up. Begin pin basting in the center of the quilt, working out to the edges. Place pins about 4" to 6" apart, being careful not to place a pin where you want to stitch.

QUILTING: The "Quilted Safari" quilt was quilted "in the ditch" fashion as shown below. Quilt along the seam lines between the blocks and along the seam lines of the borders. Quilt along the seam lines of the patchwork pieces and around the appliqué shapes.

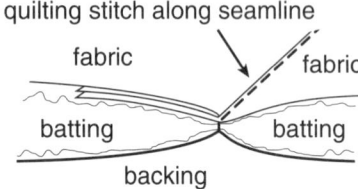

BINDING: Cut binding strips 3½" x 45". Sew the short ends of the strips together to make one long strip. Fold raw edge on short side diagonally, then fold the strip in half wrong sides together to form the binding and press. Figure A.

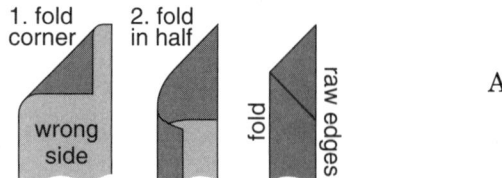

Line up the raw edges of the quilt front and the doubled raw edge of the binding and sew around the quilt beginning at the center bottom edge using ½" seam allowance. Figure B.

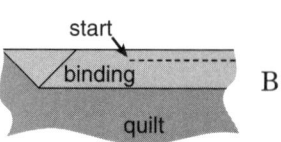

As you approach a corner, stop ½" seam allowance away from the raw edge. Figure C.

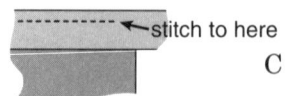

Fold the binding strip up as shown so that you have a 45° angle. Figure D.

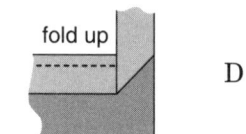

Fold the binding strip straight down making sure the raw edges of the binding are even with the raw edges of the quilt. Begin stitching ½" (seam allowance) away from the folded edge of the binding.(The stitching should meet but not overlap at the corners.) Figure E.

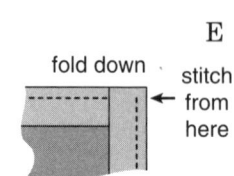

As you approach the starting point, tuck the end of the binding strip inside the folded section as shown and complete the stitching. Figure F.

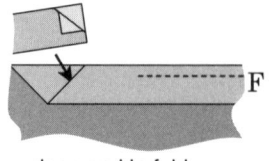

Roll the binding to the back of the quilt and hand stitch in place being sure to cover machine stitching.

HANGER: Make hanging tabs using leftover scraps of fabric. Cut three fabric strips 3" x 5". With right sides together, seam long side. Turn right side out to create a tube and press with seam open and centered on the

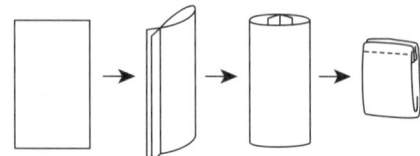

Position the tabs evenly spaced across the top of the back of the quilt (just low enough so that they cannot be seen from the front of the quilt.) Attach to the back of the quilt using hand stitching through only the backing fabric.

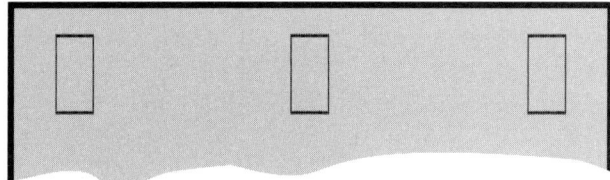

HAND EMBROIDERY STITCHES: In some of the blocks several embroidery stitches are used. Complete the stitches before putting the quilt top together.

BUTTONHOLE STITCH: Bring needle up at point 'A', down at point 'B', up again at point 'C'. Repeat down at 'B', up at 'C' until complete.

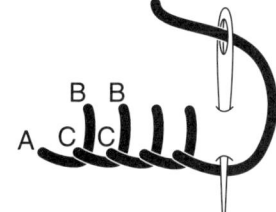

RUNNING STITCH: Bring needle up at point 'A', and down at point 'B' then back through at point 'C'. There should be a small even space between each stitch.

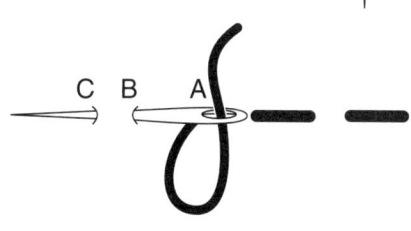

OUTLINE STITCH: Bring needle up at point 'A', down at point 'B' at a slight angle. Repeat in this manner following a designated path, such as the curved line of a branch or to outline an object.

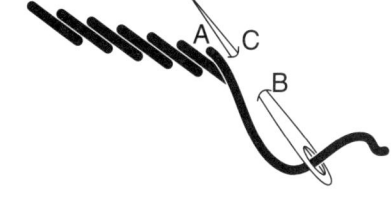

SATIN STITCH: Bring needle up at point 'A', and down at point 'B'. up again at point 'A'. Repeat in this manner until the designated area is filled in, such as a circle or a leaf. Be sure that each line of thread lies close to and even with the one before.

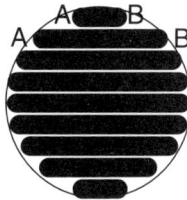

FLY STITCH: Bring needle up at point 'A', down at point 'B', up again at point 'C', then down again at point 'D'.

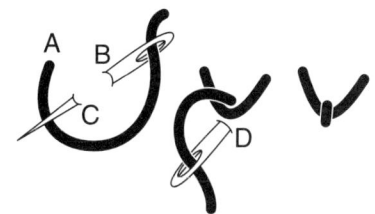

FRENCH KNOT: Bring needle up at point 'A', wrap floss around the needle two times, then bring down at 'B'.

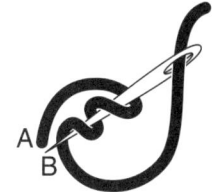

WHIP STITCH: Bring needle up at point 'A', catching a thread of the fabric on the right, then bring down at "B", again catching a stitch of the piece on the left.

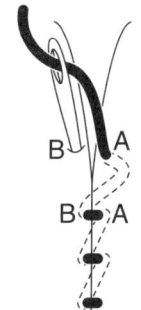

ZEBRA

Technique: Paper Piecing

Cutting Directions
Templates found on pages 36-37.

1. Cut one 12½" x 4" piece of blue floral print for sky. Cut one 12½" x 9¼" piece of beige print for ground. Trim top edge to make a slight dip in the center about ⅜" deep. Pin ground over lower edge of sky to make a 12½" square; baste along top edge of ground.

2. Cut one 12½" x 2½" piece of olive green fabric. Baste a curving line along the upper and lower edges. Trim close to the basting line with scissors.

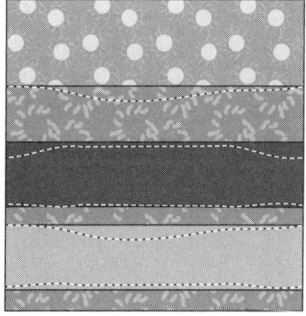

Follow steps 1-3 for cutting and placing background strips. The curved stitching lines are randomly sewn. All raw edges will be finished with the satin stitch on the sewing machine. This procedure will be used for the Elephant on page 13.

3. Cut one 12½" x 2½" piece of light blue streaked fabric. Baste a curving line along the upper and lower edges. Trim close to the basting line with scissors.

4. Cut three 1" wide strips across width of fabric from black. Cut three 1" wide strips across width of fabric from white.

Directions

1. Machine zigzag along edges of background sections matching thread to fabric.

2. Trace or photocopy front and rear zebra sections from book onto medium weight paper. Cut out sections cutting off mane, ear, and tail. Overlap and glue front and rear sections together.

3. When paper piecing, place fabric on blank side of pattern, then stitch from side with marked lines. Place a small piece of white fabric under section marked with a number 1, so it overlaps edges by at least ⅛".

4. Cut one length of black 1" strip to cover stripe below section 1. Place along lower edge of white fabric with right sides together. Stitch along line using small machine stitches, back stitching at each end. Fold fabric down over stripe marked with a dot. Dots indicate black stripes.

5. Repeat on next stripe using a piece of white fabric strip. Continue working to bottom of hind leg.

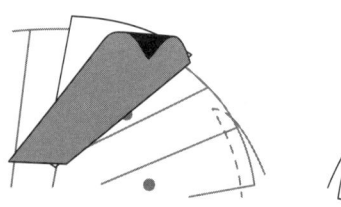 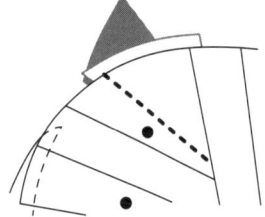

Paper Piecing the Zebra.

Trim off excess fabric along edges of paper. Then piece body from back to front continuing to last white area on head. Piece front leg last. Trim away all excess following Zebra shape.

6. Remove paper along perforations made by stitching. Pin Zebra in place on background.

7. Trace nose, tail, mane and ear onto light-weight fusible web following broken lines so pieces overlap body. Remember patterns are already reversed. Fuse ear to white fabric, and remaining pieces onto black. Cut out shapes. Position shapes in place so that they overlap to underside of Zebra's body. Fuse shapes onto block. Baste Zebra in place close to the outside edge.

8. Machine zigzag satin stitch around zebra using black thread.

LION

Technique: Paper Piecing

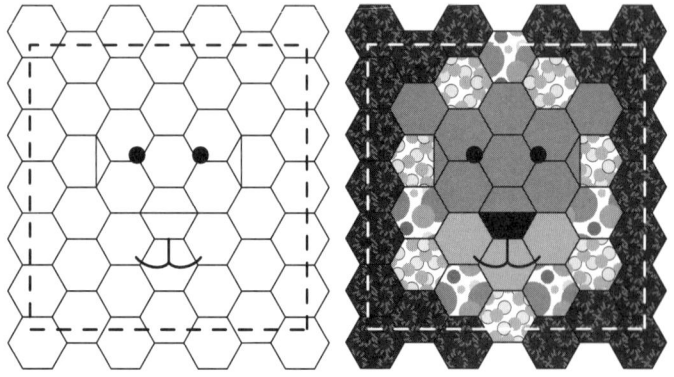

Cutting Directions
Template is found on this page.

1. Trace 46 hexagons from template below onto freezer paper and cut them out.

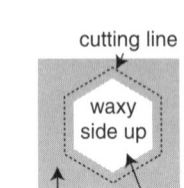

2. Lay tan fabric right side down and pin 8 hexagons with shiny, waxy side up, to the wrong side of fabric allowing about ½" margin between pieces. Cut out around each hexagon adding ¼" seam.

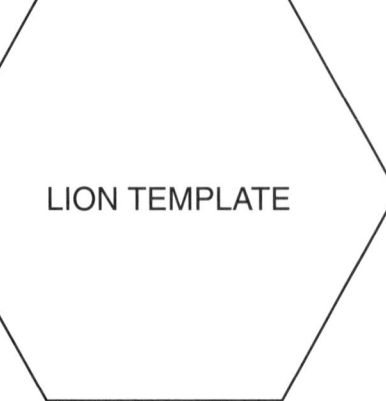

LION TEMPLATE

8

3. Place hexagons paper side up on ironing board. Carefully press seam allowance over edge of paper one side at a time. Seam allowance fabric will stick to the waxy side of the paper eliminating the need to baste under edges.

4. In the same manner make 3 off-white hexagons, 5 gold floral print hexagons, 5 gold print hexagons, and 18 purple print hexagons.

5. For nose, cut one 1½" x 3½" piece from tan and one 1½" x 3½" piece black fabric. Stitch them together along one long edge using a ¼" seam allowance. Press seam open. Pin a hexagon so that seam runs across widest point of hexagon between opposite angles, see diagram. Cut out adding ¼" seam allowance. Press under edges.

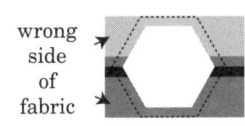

6. For sides of head, cut one 1½" x 6½" piece of tan. Cut one 2½" x 6½" piece of gold floral print. Stitch them together along one long edge using a ¼" seam allowance. Press seam open. Place hexagon over seam following diagram and pin in place. Cut out adding ¼" seam allowance. Press under edges.

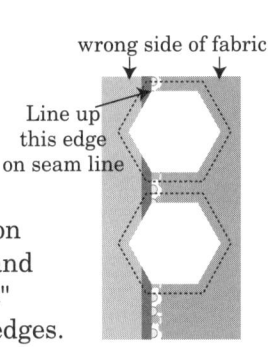

Piecing Directions

1. Place 1 off-white hexagon right sides together over nose hexagon. Join the 2 hexagons using tiny whipstitches close to the black edge of the nose. Place remaining 2 hexagons along adjacent black edges of nose and whipstitch to nose and off-white hexagons.

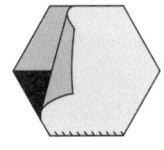

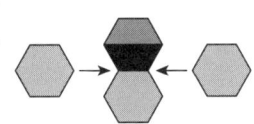

2. Stitch tan hexagons to remaining edges of nose hexagon and join them together along adjacent edges. Add 3 more tan hexagons to the tan side of this shape. Add tan hexagons for ears.

3. Stitch the gold floral/tan hexagons for the side of head below the ears. Arrange the gold print and gold floral print hexagons around the head for the mane and join them to the head and to each other.

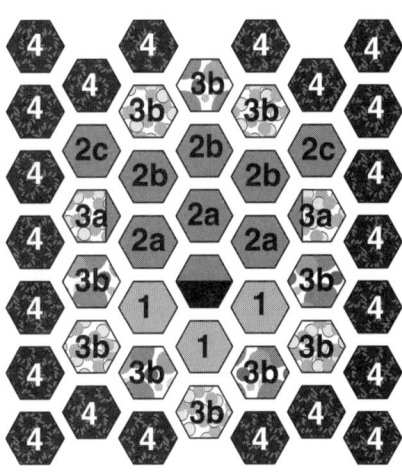

Add hexagons following steps 1-4. Numbers in the diagram refer to the piecing sequence of hexagons.

4. Cut 22 purple background hexagons and position around the head, following the placement diagram and whipstitch them to the adjacent edges. Fill in the top and bottom edges using the half hexagons.

5. Press block well from right side. Remove paper patterns. Trim side edges so block measures 12½" wide.

6. Draw mouth and embroider using black thread and narrow zigzag stitches on your sewing machine. Sew buttons to positions for eyes.

GIRAFFE

Technique: Reverse Appliqué

Cutting Directions
Templates are found on page 30.

1. Cut one 6½" x 12½" piece of blue streaked fabric. Make a template by tracing giraffe. Trace giraffe to center of fabric. Cut out center of giraffe about ¼" inside the drawn line.

2. Cut one 6" x 12" piece of solid tan or geometric tan print. Place under center of blue fabric with both fabrics right side up. Baste fabrics together about ½" outside drawn lines.

3. Cut two 3½" x 12½" pieces from magenta print. Make a template for leaves. Arrange leaves on template following placement diagram leaving about ½" margin around edge of fabric. Trace leaves onto print pieces. Cut out centers of leaves about ¼" inside the drawn line.

4. Cut two 3" x 12" piece of solid green fabric. Place under center of magenta print with both fabrics right side up. Baste fabrics together between drawn lines of leaves.

Directions

1. To reverse appliqué the giraffe, turn under the edges of the blue streaked fabric along the drawn line of the giraffe using your fingers or the tip of your needle. Slipstitch them in place as you go. Clip seam allowance for smooth turning along curves and at points. If seam allowance is scant use tiny whip stitches to finish the edges. When stitching is finished, trim excess tan fabric about ¼" from stitching on wrong side.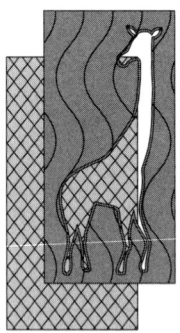

2. Embroider the horns using brown satin stitches. Embroider the tail using brown outline stitches and satin stitches. Embroider the hooves using black satin stitch. then embroider the eye in black, using outline stitch and satin stitch. Make a small fly stitch in black for the nose.

3. To reverse appliqué the leaves, turn under the edges of the magenta print along the drawn line of the leaves following the instructions given above. Trim excess green fabric about ¼" from stitching on wrong side.

4. Stitch side panels with leaves to each side of giraffe panel.

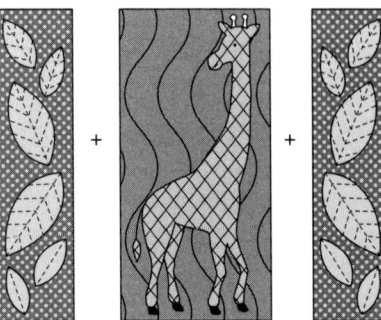

FISH
Technique: Eight Pointed Star

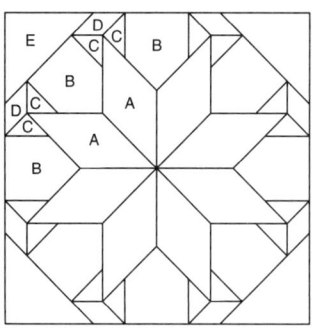 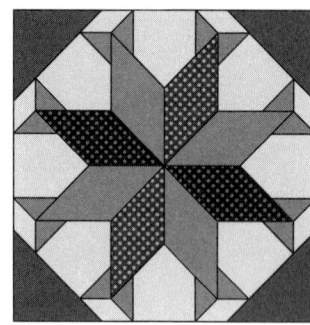

Cutting Directions
Templates are found on page 32.

1. Adding ¼" seam allowance to all pieces: Cut 4 large diamonds (A) and 8 small triangles (C) from gold print. Cut 2 large diamonds (A) and 4 small triangles (C) from each purple and magenta prints.

2. From aqua print, cut 8 background pieces (B) and 8 small diamonds (D).

3. Cut 4 large triangles from blue streaked fabric.

Directions

1. Stitch a magenta or purple diamond to each gold diamond along one edge so that the gold diamond is to the right side of the pair.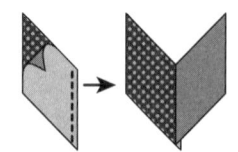
Begin stitching at edge of center point and end ¼" in at side corner of the stitching line. Backstitch to secure. Trim seam allowance at center point of diamond. Press seam allowance toward gold diamond.

2. Stitch pairs of diamonds together alternating colors and joining them as in step 1.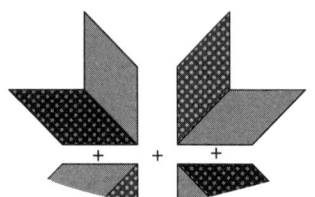

3. Arrange diamonds as they appear in the block. Matching colors, stitch small triangles (C) along sides of background piece (B) to make the tail fins.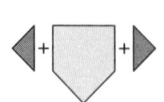

4. Stitch B-C units between outer points of diamonds matching colors. Begin stitch at side corner of diamonds and end ¼" in at outer point.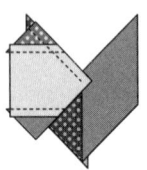

10

5. Stitch small diamonds (D) to outer edges of tail fins to complete an octagon shape.
6. Stitch large triangles (E) to corners to form a square.

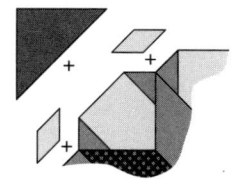

KANGAROO

Technique: Paper Piecing

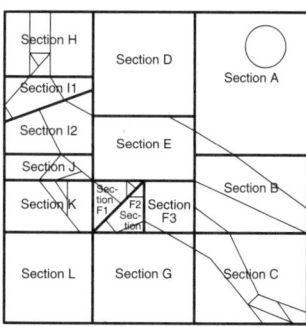 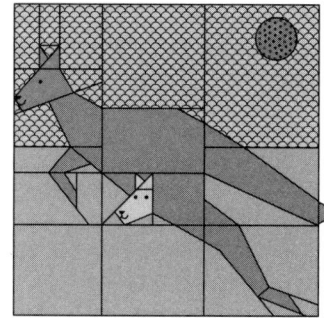

Cutting and Piecing Directions
Templates are found on pages 38-40.

1. Trace or photocopy paper piecing patterns from this book. Cut out each paper section.

2. To make this block, you will need blue floral print, rust, tan print, and a small piece of gold solid fabric. Follow the colors indicated on the patterns. Place a piece of the fabric indicated (right side down) under the piece in each paper section marked with a 1. Pin in place.

3. (NOTE: Refer to paper piecing graphic for Zebra.) Place a piece of the color fabric indicated for area section 2 right sides together along the seam line between sections 1 and 2. Stitch along the seam line through both layers of fabric from the printed side of the pattern backstitching at the beginning and end of the seam.

4. Trim seam allowance to ³⁄₁₆" from stitching. Fold fabric over seam to cover section 2.

5. Continue adding fabric to cover each section in the same manner following numerical order.

6. On pattern C, to cover sections 5 and 6 place fabric along longer seam line of section and stitch to dot. Fold fabric over seam to cover section. Trim fabric and turn under ³⁄₁₆" along remaining seam line and slipstitch in place.

7. Carefully press each pattern and remove paper backing along perforations made by stitching.

8. In addition to the patterns given, cut one 4½" square of blue floral print for D and one 4" square of tan print for L.

9. Stitch F1 to F2. Then stitch this piece to F3. Stitch I1 to I2.

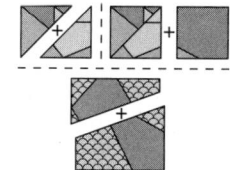

10. Stitch A, B and C together to make a vertical row. Then Join D-G for center of block. Stitch remaining pieces together.

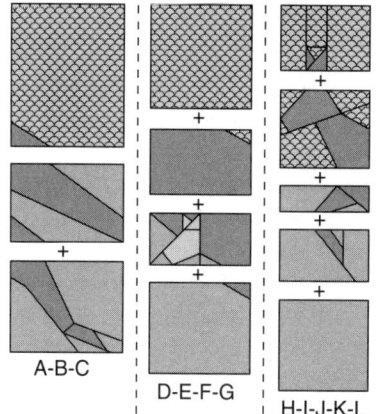

A-B-C   D-E-F-G   H-I-J-K-L

11. Join the rows to make a block matching seams of kangaroo's body.

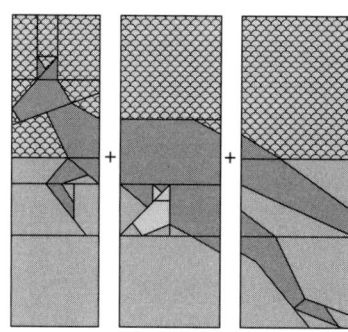

12. Cut one circle for the sun from freezer paper. Fuse to wrong side of gold print fabric. Cut out fabric ³⁄₁₆" bigger than paper. Turn under edges of fabric over paper and baste edge in place. Slip-stitch sun to sky on pattern A. Make a small slit in background fabric under appliqué and remove paper pattern.

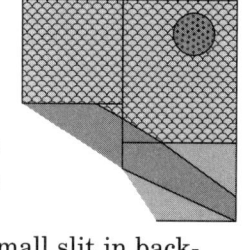

13. Fold tail in half. Stitch along seam line of long raw edge. Trim seam line at point of tail. Turn right side out. Right sides together stitch to side of block at end of tail. Embroider eyes and noses in satin stitch with black floss. Embroider mouth in outline stitch with black floss. After sashing is attached, fold tail over sashing and stitch in place.

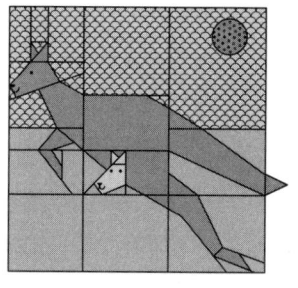

TURTLE

Technique: Curved Hand Piecing

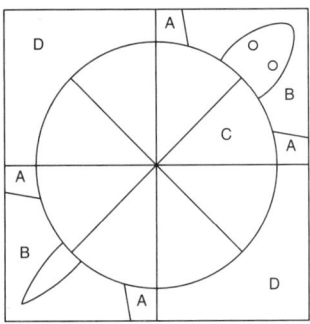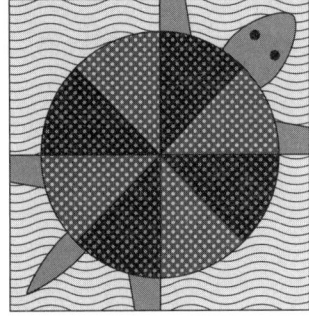

Cutting Directions
Templates are found on pages 36-37.

1. Add ¼" seam allowance to all pieces. Cut from light blue streaked fabric 2 pieces B and 2 pieces D. Trace seam line to wrong side of pieces along inner curves. If fabric is directional make sure design on all pieces is going in the same direction. (See water print in color illustration on cover.)

2. Cut 4 legs (A) from brown.

3. Cut 4 each shell pieces (C) from green print and 4 from dark green print.

4. Trace head and tail to freezer paper. Cut out. Fuse to wrong side of brown fabric. Cut out, adding scant ¼" seam allowance.

Directions

1. Stitch a leg (A) to each side of background section B. Appliqué head and tail in center of each background section B.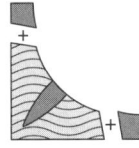

2. Stitch each green shell piece to a dark green shell piece.

3. Clip inner curve of A-B and D background pieces. Matching edges and center, stitch shell sections to background pieces by hand.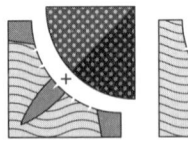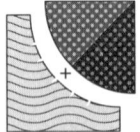

4. Arrange pieces to form block. Stitch pieces together in pairs to make half blocks. Stitch half blocks together, matching seams. Add buttons for eyes.

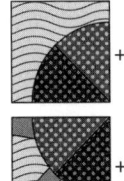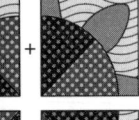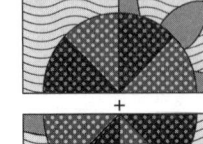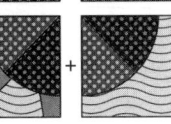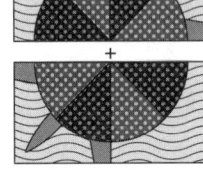

CAT

Technique: Hand/Machine Piecing

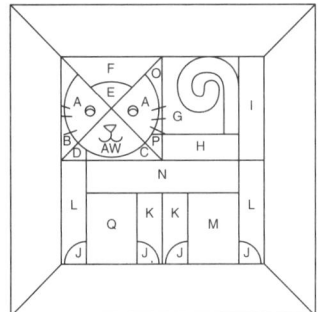

Cutting Directions
Templates are found on page 33.

1. Adding ¼" seam allowance, make templates for pattern pieces.

2. From black use templates to cut 2 face pieces A, 1 face piece E, 2 paws J, 1 section C and 1 section P. Then cut one 3" x 2½" piece for leg piece M, a 2" x 6½" piece body section N and 3½" x 1½" piece for H (these pieces include seam allowance.)

3. Trace tail to freezer paper and fuse to wrong side of black. Cut out adding ¼" around paper.

4. From white use templates to cut 1 face section AW and 2 paws J. Then cut a 3" x 2½" piece for leg piece Q (these pieces include seam allowance.)

5. From gold print use templates to cut 1 B piece, 1 O piece, 1 D piece, and 1 F piece; cut 1 each of pieces K and L, reverse patterns and cut another K and L. Then cut one 3½" square for piece G and one 4½" x 1½" piece for I (these pieces include seam allowance.)

6. Using template, cut two borders from dark green print and two borders from magenta print.

Directions

1. Stitch black C to gold D. Stitch gold O to black P.

2. Mark seam line along curves on pieces A, B, C-D, E and F, AW and O-P. Clip seam allowance along curves on B, C-D and F. Arrange pieces for the cat's face following piecing diagram. Matching centers and raw edges, stitch black A to B, white AW to C-D, black A to O-P and E to F by hand using tiny running stitches, creating 4 triangles.

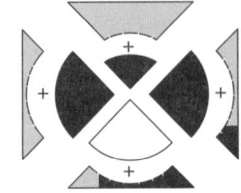

3. Stitch triangles together in pairs. Then stitch larger triangles together matching center seams to make face square.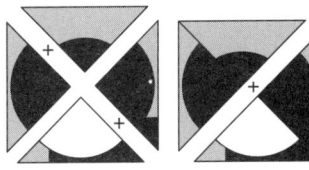

4. Turn under curved edges of tail to wrong side of paper pattern. Press and remove paper. Appliqué tail to piece G.

5. Stitch H to lower edge of G. Stitch I to G-H. Stitch this piece to head matching seams of body to make top of cat.

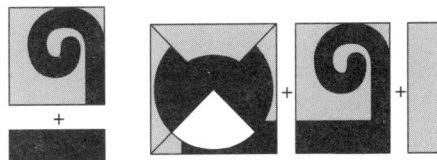

6. Mark seam line along curves on pieces J, K and L just as you did in step 2. Clip seam allowance along curves on K and L pieces. Matching centers and raw edges, sew white J pieces to K and L for back paws. Sew black pieces to K and L for front paws.

7. Stitch J-K pieces together for center of lower edge (a). Stitch white legs M to left edge of center and stitch black legs Q to right edge of center (b). Stitch body piece N to top (c). Stitch J-L pieces to sides to make bottom of cat (d).

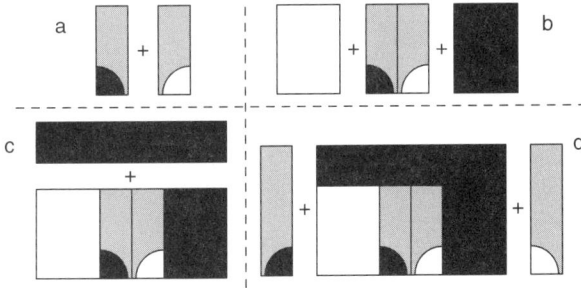

8. Stitch top and bottom of cat together matching seams.

9. Stitch magenta borders to top and bottom beginning and ending ¼" in from edges.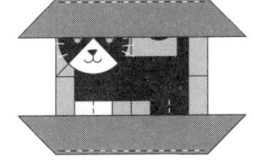

Stitch green borders to sides beginning and ending ¼" in from edges.

Following the diagram below, stitch borders together at corners. Border strips are at 45° angles to each other, right sides together.

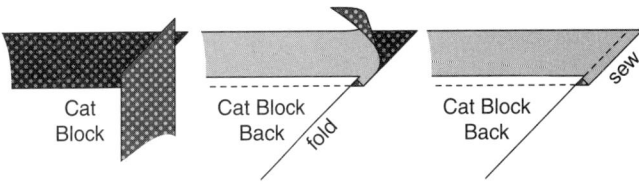

ELEPHANTS

Technique: Machine Appliqué

 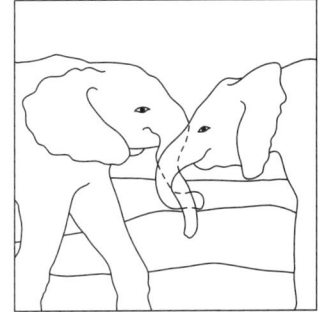

Cutting Directions
Templates are found on pages 26-27.

(NOTE: Refer to Zebra for completing background sections.)

1. Cut one 12½" x 8" piece of light blue streaked fabric for sky.

2. Cut one 12½" x 5½" piece of beige print for ground. Trim top edge to make a slight dip in the center about ⅜" deep. Pin ground over lower edge of sky to make a 12½" square; baste along top edge of ground.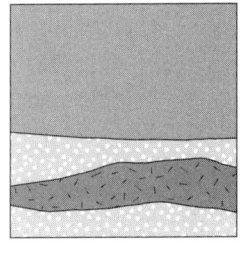

3. Cut one 12½" x 2½" piece of olive green print. Trim long edges to make a curved irregular shape. Pin across ground area as shown in the diagram. Baste upper and lower edges in place.

4. Trace elephant patterns to fusible web. Patterns are already reversed. Fuse to wrong side of gray fabric. Cut out elephants. Place elephants on background intertwining their trunks. Fuse them in place. Transfer detail lines for legs, ears, mouth, etc. to elephants.

Directions

1. Using matching thread, machine satin stitch along raw edges of background pieces, and the outlines and detail lines of elephants.

2. Embroider eyes of elephant by hand using black outline stitch along upper edge, black satin stitch for pupil and fill in around pupil with brown satin stitch.

SHEEP AND DUCKS

Technique: Biscuit Square

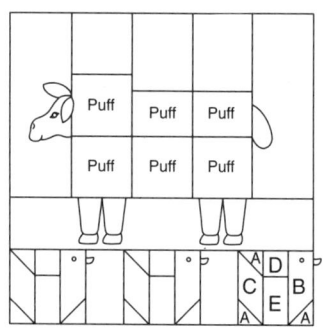 

Cutting Directions
Templates are found on page 33.

1. Make templates for ducks by tracing patterns. Add ¼" seam allowance around pieces.

2. From white, cut four 2⅞" squares and four 3½" squares. Cut two rectangles 2" x 2⅞" and two rectangles 2½" x 3½".

3. From blue leaf print, cut two pieces 7¾" x 2⅞", two pieces 2⅞" x 3½" and a 2⅞" square.

4. From green print, cut one 12½" x 2½" large rectangle, two 3½" x 2" medium rectangle, three small squares D and nine small triangles A.

5. From gold print, cut three diamonds C, three small rectangles E and three heads B.

6. Trace appliqué pieces for sheep's head, ears, tail, legs and hooves in reverse. Cut out pieces. Press head and hooves to black and remaining pieces to white. Cut out, adding ¼" around edges of paper. Press edges that won't be overlapped in seam allowances, remove paper and baste in place.

Piecing Directions

1. Pin large white squares to top of small white squares at corners. Fold extra fabric flat to make a right to left pleat in center of side on three edges of square. Insert a small amount of stuffing inside squares. Pin a pleat in remaining side. Baste squares together around edges to make a "biscuit". Assemble small and large rectangles to make "biscuits" in same manner.

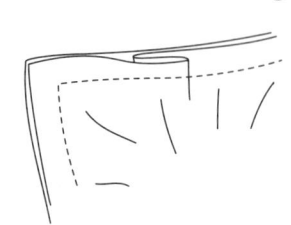

2. Stitch each rectangular biscuit to top edge of a square biscuit then stitch a small blue rectangle to the top of each rectangular biscuit. Stitch two square biscuits together. Stitch a blue square to top edge. Stitch these three sections together.

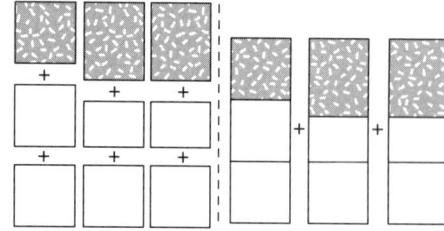

4. Position large blue rectangles on either side of body. Place head, ears and tail to position on rectangles. Appliqué pieces in place. Stitch to sides of body.

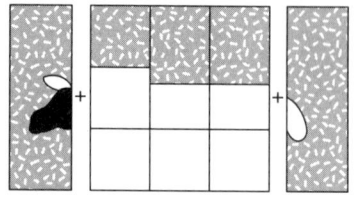

5. Position large green rectangle below body. Place legs and hooves in position on rectangle. Slipstitch pieces in place. Remove basting. Stitch to lower edge of body and sky.

6. Stitch a small triangle A to lower edge of each head piece B. Stitch small triangles to edges of each diamond C to make a rectangle. Stitch squares D to E. Stitch sections together to make ducks.

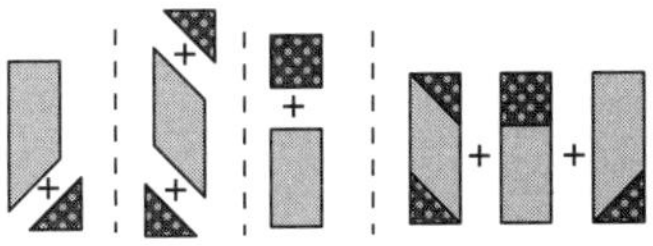

7. Stitch a medium rectangle to each side of one duck. Join remaining ducks to opposite sides of rectangle. Sew to lower edge of sheep.

8. Embroider eyes using black satin stitch and beaks using gold satin stitch. (Right duck's beak must be embroidered after sashing is attached.)

WOODLAND ANIMALS

Technique: Buttonhole Stitch Appliqué

Cutting and Piecing Directions
Templates are found on pages 34-35.

1. Cut one 12½ x 3" piece of blue leaf print for sky.

2. Trace patterns for hills from book. Cut hills #1 and #4 from dark green leaf print. Cut hill #2 from olive print. Cut hill #3 from green print. Turn pieces wrong side up. Place fusible web over top edge of hill; trace along top. Draw another parallel line about ¼" below top edge to make a narrow strip. Cut out strip. Fuse to wrong side of each hill.

3. Trace squirrel, moose, antlers, bear and rabbit patterns from book. Reverse patterns and trace them to fusible web. Fuse squirrel to wrong side of gray fabric, Moose to dark brown, antlers to tan, bear to rust brown, and rabbit to light brown. Cut out each piece.

Piecing Directions

1. Place sky on ironing board. Place hill #1 even with left side of sky about 1" below top edge. Place hill #2 even with right edge about 1" below top edge. Place hills #3 and #4 below to complete a 12½" square. Use a ruler to check the size of the square. Fuse the pieces together along the top edge of the hills.

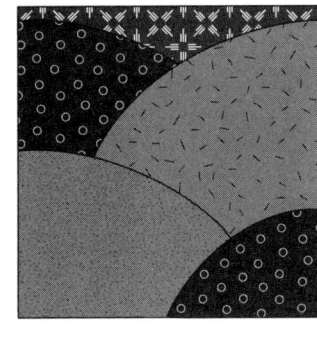

2. Place the animals on each hill following the patterns and fuse them in place.

3. Using buttonhole stitch, stitch along edges of hills and animals using 4 strands of gold, gray, brown, dark brown and rust embroidery floss. Embroider eyes using dark brown satin stitch. Stitch rabbit's tail with off-white French knots.

15

PANDA

Technique: Machine Piecing

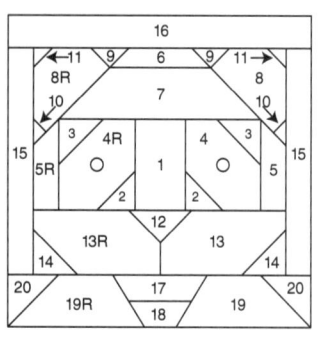 

Cutting
Templates are found on pages 31-32.

NOTE: When cutting pieces designated with "R" they must be cut in reverse so their orientation in the block will be correct.

1. From white, cut one center section 1, two each triangles 2 and 3, one side piece 5 and one side piece 5R, one head piece 7, one lower face piece 13 and one lower face 13R, and one chin 17.

2. From black, one eye shape 4 and one eye shape 4R, one ear piece 8 and one ear piece 8R, one nose 12, one center body 18, and one body piece 19 and one body piece 19R.

3. From blue floral print, cut two each of small background triangles 9, 10 and 11, two triangles 14, two 9¼" x 1½" rectangles for piece 15, one 12½" x 1¾" rectangle for piece 16, two triangles 20, and 1 piece 6.

Piecing Directions

1. Stitch white triangles 2 and 3 to black eye shape 4. Be sure to make a left and right piece. Stitch these units to each side of center section 1, then stitch section 5 to outer edges.

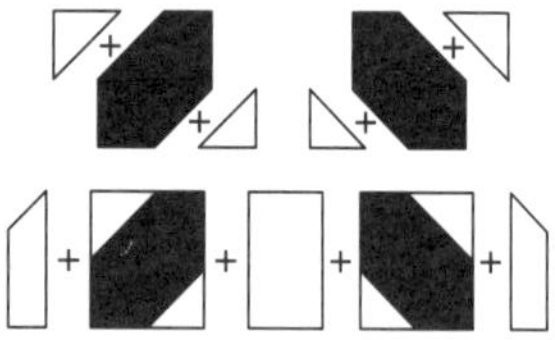

2. Stitch upper head piece 7 to top of unit 1-5. Stitch background piece 6 to top of head.

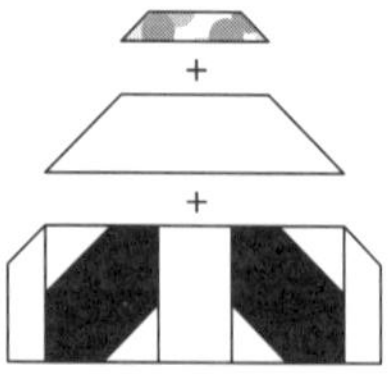

3. Stitch small background triangle 9, 10 and 11 to ear piece 8. Be sure to make a left and right ear. Stitch this unit to diagonal edge of head.

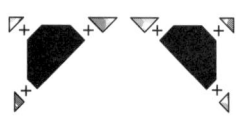 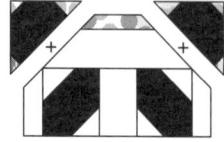

4. Stitch lower face pieces 13 and 13R together along center, beginning stitching ¼" in from top edge as shown in the graphic that follows.

Stitch nose 12 to top center edges of lower face. Place nose right sides together with the left face section and stitch from outer edge to seam intersection of face.

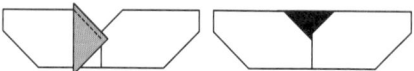

Turn nose section so that it is now right sides together with right face section. Stitch from outer edge to seam intersection of face.

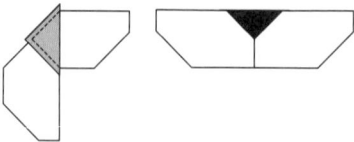

5. Stitch background triangle 14 to diagonal edge of lower face. Stitch this section to lower edge of unit 1-5.

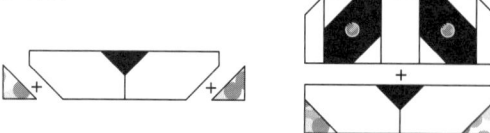

6. Stitch small narrow strip 15 to each side of face. Stitch large narrow strip 16 to top edge.

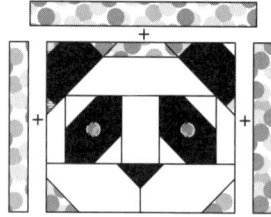

7. Stitch chin 17 and center body 18 together. Stitch body piece 19 and 19R to each side of unit 17-18. Stitch background triangle 20 to sides to complete the rectangle. Stitch to bottom edge of face.

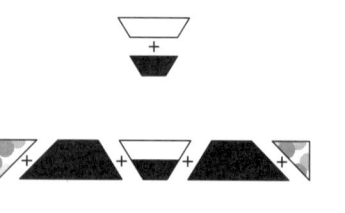 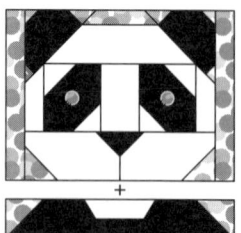

8. Draw mouth and embroider using black thread and narrow zigzag stitches on your sewing machine. Sew buttons to positions for eyes.

PARROT

Technique: Appliqué

Cutting
Templates are found on pages 28-29.

1. Trace design elements for parrot block: body, wings, head, branch and leaves to make a full size pattern for block on a 12½" square of paper. Cut one 12½" square of lavender print fabric. Trace outline of shapes onto fabric.

2. Trace each appliqué shape, branch, leaves, feet, legs, body, wing feathers, head, eye, beak pieces, etc. in reverse on freezer paper. Cut out shapes. Fuse to color indicated in photo or graphic. Cut out shapes adding 3/16" around outer edge of paper. Fold fabric edges over edge of paper and baste edges in place that will not be overlapped by other shapes.

3. Make template for tail feathers. Trace template onto 2 layers of fabric with right sides together. Make two magenta print, three blue leaf print, two gold floral print and two purple print.

4. Cut one small triangle of blue leaf print to cover area on background between legs and branch.

Directions

1. Stitch around traced lines of tail feathers leaving an opening on side near point for turning. Trim edges to ⅛" from stitching. Clip seam allowance. Turn right side out. Slipstitch openings. Press feathers flat.

2. Place one red tail feather in center of area between legs. Stitch top of feather in place.

3. Pin branch in place. Pin two blue feathers under branch. Trim top edge of feathers above placement line of branch to remove bulk. Stitch top of blue feathers in place. Slipstitch branch and leaves in place using matching thread.

4. Appliqué legs, feet and body in place. Pin wing feathers in place and slipstitch edges.

5. Pin head pieces and beak in place and slipstitch.

6. Remove basting on appliqué pieces. Trim away background fabric behind appliqué pieces and remove paper patterns.

7. Embroider eye using black satin stitches. Mark quilting design on body.

8. When sashing is complete, arrange remaining tail feathers and stitch top edge of feathers to quilt top.

SAFARI WALL HANGING

Approximate size: 41½" x 41½"

Materials:

45" wide cotton fabrics
¾ yard red floral print (includes binding)
⅜ yard tan geometric print
⅜ yard dark brown animal skin print
⅛ yard tan leopard skin print
¾ yard animal print (1 yard if fabric has vertical design)
⅛ yard white
⅛ yard or 3" x 9" scrap cream
¼ yard tan
¼ yard grey
⅛ yard gold
⅛ yard gold print
1¼ yards fabric for backing
44" square Poly-fil® Low-Loft® quilt batting
Thread to match fabrics
½ yard paper backed fusible web
Invisible nylon thread for machine quilting

Directions

Refer to the blocks in the front portion of the book for complete piecing instructions.

Zebra

1. Cut a 9½" x 12½" piece from red floral print. Cut two 2" x 12½" strips from tan geometric print.

2. Stitch tan strips to top and bottom edges of red floral piece to make background.

3. Make zebra and appliqué it to background following directions on pages 7-8.

Lion

Cut and make lion block following instructions on pages 8-9. Substitute tan leopard print for purple print in background. Substitute solid gold fabric for gold print and gold print for gold floral print. Follow directions for appliqué eyes.

Elephants

1. Cut a 12½" square of dark brown animal skin print for background.

2. Cut and appliqué elephants on background following directions on pages 13-14.

Giraffe

1. Cut a 6½" x 12½" piece of red floral print. Cut two 3½" x 12½" pieces from tan geometric print.

2. Stitch tan pieces to side edges of red floral print to make background.

3. Trace giraffe, tail, and hooves in reverse on paper backed fusible webbing. Fuse giraffe and tail to wrong side of tan fabric. Fuse hooves to black. Cut out pieces.

4. Fuse giraffe to center of red floral piece. Zigzag around appliqué pieces using matching thread. Zigzag stitch line of tail.

5. Embroider the horns using brown satin stitches. Embroider the eye in black, using outline stitch and satin stitch. Make a small fly stitch in black for the nose.

6. Lightly draw diamond pattern on body as shown in the photo. Stitch around diamonds by machine using brown straight stitches.

Cutting Sashing and Borders

1. From black, cut two 27½" x 2" strips for top and bottom, three 26" x 2" vertical strips and two 12½" x 2" strips.

2. Cut four 6¾" corner squares from dark brown animal skin print.

3. From animal print, cut four 27½" x 6¾" border strips. If fabric is directional, cut two border strips across the fabric and two border strips lengthwise on the fabric.

Assembling

Refer to pages 5-7 for finishing information.

1. Stitch zebra block and elephant block to top and bottom of a short sashing strip to join them. Join lion block and giraffe block in same manner.

2. Stitch pairs of blocks to opposite sides of one vertical sashing strip. Stitch remaining vertical sashing strips to side edges of quilt.

3. Stitch long sashing strips to top and bottom of center.

4. Stitch border strips to side edges of quilt.

5. Stitch a corner square to each end of remaining border strips. Stitch these borders to top and bottom edges of quilt matching seams.

6. To make backing, cut selvedges from backing fabric.

7. Following directions for *"Quilted Safari"* sampler quilt, assemble wall hanging, batting and backing.

8. Quilt "in the ditch" along outlines of animals and seams of blocks, sashing strips and borders. Quilt around outline of printed animals on borders.

9. Cut a 40" x 7" strip to make a casing to hang the wall hanging. Fold strip in half lengthwise and stitch across ends using a ¼" seam allowance. Turn right side out. Baste to wrong side matching raw edge to top edge of wall hanging. Slipstitch fold to backing of wall hanging.

10. Make a 3½" wide binding 172" long using red print fabric. Bind edges of wall hanging using ½" seam allowance following directions on page 6.

COUNT THE ANIMALS WALL HANGING

Approximate size: 25" x 53"

Materials:

45" wide cotton fabrics
1⅜ yard royal blue print
⅜ yard yellow
⅛ yard black
⅛ yard white
⅛ yard fushia dot
⅝ yard turquoise
¼ yard or 6" x 12" square yellow dot
¼ yard or 6" x 12" square orange dot
⅛ yard royal blue dot
⅛ yard lime green
⅛ yard kelly green
⅛ yard brown
1⅝ yard backing fabric
58" x 30" piece Poly-fil® Traditional® quilt batting
Two ½" diameter black and white variegated buttons
Six 6mm diameter brown beads
Black, yellow and pink embroidery floss
Thread to match fabrics
Invisible nylon thread for machine quilting
Pink, orange and turquoise acrylic fabric paint
Stencil for 1" high block letters and numbers
Stenciling brush
Masking tape

Directions

Panda

Following directions on page 16, make panda block substituting fushia dot for blue floral print.

Giraffes

1. Cut a 12½" square piece of turquoise fabric. Fold square in half vertically and mark center. Make a template by tracing giraffe pattern on page 30. Trace giraffe centered on left side of fabric. Reverse template and trace giraffe centered on right side of fabric. Cut out centers of giraffes about ⅛" inside the drawn line.

2. Cut a 6" x 12" piece of each yellow dot and orange dot. Place yellow dot under center of left giraffe with both fabrics right side up. Place orange dot under center of right giraffe with both fabrics right side up. Baste layers of fabrics together about ½" outside drawn lines.

3. Reverse appliqué the giraffes following the directions for "*Quilted Safari*" sampler quilt on page 10.

4. For both giraffes, embroider the hooves using black satin stitch. Then embroider the eye in black, using outline stitch and satin stitch. Make a small fly stitch in black for the nose.

5. For the yellow giraffe, embroider the horns using pink satin stitches. Embroider the tail using black outline stitches and pink satin stitches.

6. For the orange giraffe, embroider the horns using yellow satin stitches. Embroider the tail using black outline stitches and yellow satin stitches.

Turtles

Cutting

1. Make templates for the small turtle blocks by tracing the patterns on page 28.

2. Cut 6 each of background pieces B and D from royal blue dot fabric. Trace seamline to wrong side of pieces along inner curves. If fabric is directional, make sure designs on all pieces are going in the same direction. Cut two 6½" x 3½" rectangles from royal blue dot.

3. Cut 12 each shell pieces (C) from lime green, and kelly green fabrics.

4. Trace 3 heads and 3 tails to freezer paper. Cut out. Fuse to wrong side of brown fabric. Cut out adding ³⁄₁₆" seam allowance.

Directions

1. Following directions for the turtle block of the "*Quilted Safari*" sampler quilt on page 12, make 3 small turtle blocks.

2. Arrange the blocks with the turtles heads and tails pointing in the directions shown in the diagram or photo.

3. Stitch the two turtles on the left side together. Stitch the rectangles to the top and bottom of the remaining turtle. Stitch the two halves of the block together.

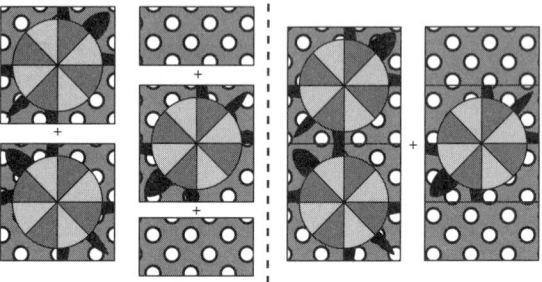

4. Sew small beads to position for eyes.

Cutting Sashing and Borders

1. From yellow, cut two sashing strips 12½" x 2½", two top and bottom strips 16½" x 2½" and two side sashing pieces 40½" x 2½".

2. From royal blue print, cut two side borders 44½" x 4¾" and two top and bottom borders 25" x 4¾".

Assembling

1. Stencil the words "1 PANDA" on one 12½" long sashing strip using orange paint. Stencil the words "2 GIRAFFES" on the other 12½" long sashing strip using fushia paint. Stencil the words "3 TURTLES" on one 16½" long sashing strip using turquoise paint. Allow paint to dry.

2. Assemble the wallhanging in the same manner as the quilt. Refer to the directions for sashing on page 5. Stitch "1 PANDA" sashing strip to lower edge of panda block. Stitch "2 GIRAFFES" sashing strip to lower edge of giraffe block. Stitch top edge of giraffe block to remaining edge of panda sashing strip. Stitch turtle block to lower edge of giraffe sashing strip.

3. Stitch side sashing strips to side edges of blocks. Stitch plain strip to top and "3 TURTLES" strip to lower edge of turtle block.

4. Stitch side borders to sides of quilt center. Stitch top and bottom borders to top and bottom of quilt.

5. Cut a 30" x 60" piece from backing fabric.

6. Following directions for "*Quilted Safari*" sampler quilt, assemble wall hanging, batting and backing.

7. Quilt "in the ditch" along outlines of animals and seams of blocks, sashing strips and borders. Quilt around the center or the border

8. Cut a 23" x 7" strip to make a casing to hang the wall hanging. Fold strip in half lengthwise and stitch across ends using a ¼" seam allowance. Turn right side out. Baste to wrong side matching raw edge to top edge of wall hanging. Slipstitch fold to backing of wall hanging.

10. Make a 3½" wide binding 160" long using turquoise fabric. Bind edges of wall hanging using ½" seam allowance following directions on page 6.

TURTLE AND FISH PILLOW

Materials:

45" wide cotton fabrics
⅛ yard green
½ yard green print
¼ yard floral print
¼ yard blue print
⅛ yard light blue floral print
⅛ yard brown
½ yard gold print
⅛ yard bright pink print
¾ yard fabric for pillow back
30" square backing for pillow top
30" square Poly-fil® Low-Loft® quilt batting
Two ¼" diameter brown buttons
Sewing thread to match fabrics
Invisible nylon thread for machine quilting
3 yards ⅝" diameter cotton cording
30" Poly-fil® Pop-in-Pillow® insert or Poly-fil® polyester fiberfill

Cutting

Turtle

1. Following directions on page 12, cut turtle block substituting solid green for green print, green print for dark green print and blue print for streaked fabric.

Fish

1. From floral print, cut 8 triangles (F).

2. From gold print cut 4 large diamonds (A) and 8 small triangles (C). From magenta print cut 4 large diamonds (A) and 8 small triangles (C).

3. From light blue floral print, cut 4 background pieces (B), 8 background pieces (G), 8 small diamonds (D) and 8 rectangles 4⅞" by 2¼" (H).

4. From green print fabric, cut 2 border strips 22" x 2¾" and 2 border strips 27" x 2¾" and 4 large triangles.

5. From gold print, cut 3" wide bias strips to cover 3 yards of cording.

6. For pillow back cut a 24½" x 27" piece and a 10½" x 27" piece.

Directions

1. Assemble turtle block following directions on page 12.

2. Assemble fish sections following the diagrams and directions that follow:

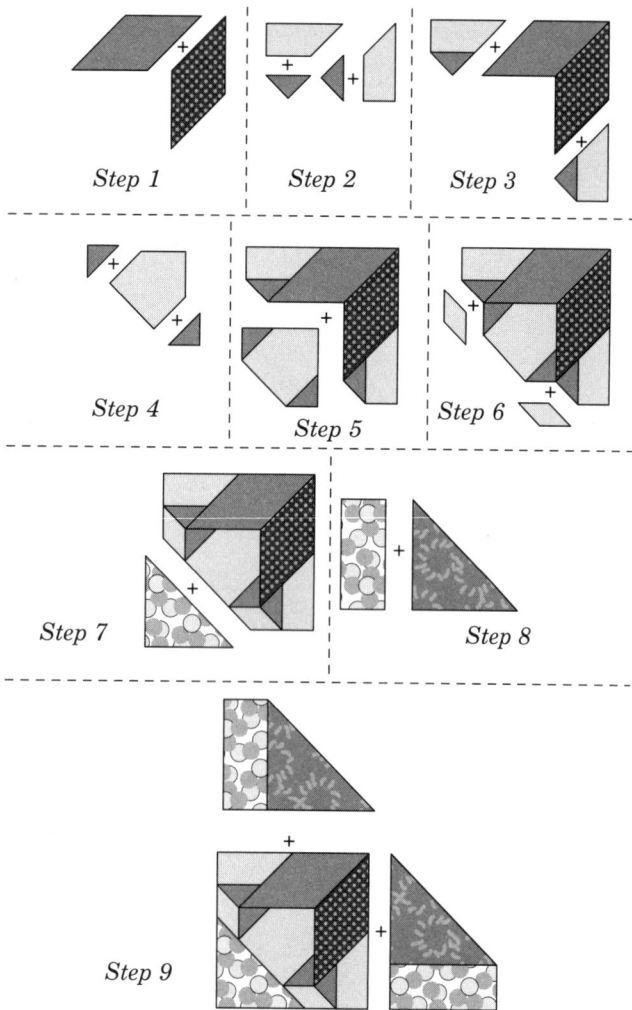

1) Stitch 2 (A) diamonds together beginning at edge of center point and ending ¼" in at side corner. Make four sets.

2) Stitch piece (G) and piece (C) together. Make 8 sets.

3) Attach piece C-G to sides of diamonds. Make 4.

4) Attach piece (C) to sides of piece (B). Make 4.

5) Set-in piece C-B to unit completed in step 3. Follow set-in technique for the fish block found on page 10. Make 4.

6) Set-in small diamonds (D) to unit completed in step 5. Follow set-in technique for fish block.

7) Attach triangle (E). Make 4.

8) Stitch triangle (F) to rectangle (H). Make 4.

9) Attach unit F-H to fish square. Make 4.

3. Attach corner units completed in (9) to sides of turtle block.

4. Stitch short border strips to opposite edges of pillow center. Then stitch longer border strips to remaining edges of pillow.

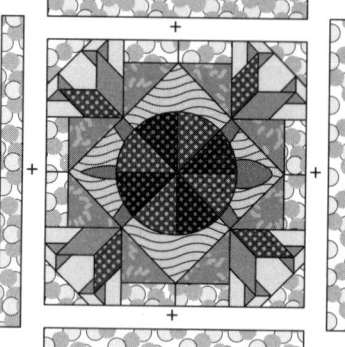

Assembling Pillow

1. Place batting between the patchwork pillow top and the backing for pillow top with right sides out. Pin or baste layers together.

2. Quilt along the seams of the patchwork pieces.

3. Sew buttons to position on turtles head for eyes.

4. Sew ends of gold print bias strips together on straight grain to make covering for cording. Fold long bias strip in half lengthwise inserting cording along the fold. With raw edges even pin then baste along edge of cording using a zipper foot.

5. Using a ½" seam allowance, stitch cording around right side of pillow top matching raw edges. Clip seam allowance of cording at corners. Join ends of cording neatly.

6. Turn under 1" then 1" again along one 27" edge of each backing piece. Stitch hems in along edge.

7. Place hemmed edge of larger back piece over hemmed edge of shorter piece to make a 27" square. Baste pieces together ½" from edges. Right sides together, stitch pillow top to pillow back using a zipper foot and stitching just inside basting. Add a second row of stitching for reinforcement, if desired.

8. Turn right side out. Insert pillow.

GIRL'S CAT JACKET

Materials

⅜ yard brightly colored cat print fabric
¼ yard coordinating print fabric
½ yard striped fabric
½ yard fushia dot fabric
¼ yard each orange and yellow dot fabric
¼ yard green star print
⅛ yard lime green
⅛ yard turquoise
⅛ yard purple
2" square scrap of bright pink
1¼ yard lining fabric
45" x 45" piece Soft Touch® cotton batting
Six ½"-⅝" diameter buttons
Six ⅜" diameter buttons for cat eyes
Black embroidery floss
Paper, pencil and ruler to make pattern

Pattern

Note: If you have difficulty determining ease or placement of neckline, armhole, etc., use an oversize sweatshirt or jacket that fits your child to compare measurements and shapes.

1. Measure chest and add 4" ease. Divide this measurement in half to determine width. Measure desired length of jacket.

2. To make back, draw a rectangle the desired length by half the chest measurement including ease. Mark vertical center back. Measure width of neck and mark in center of upper edge of rectangle. If desired, slope shoulder seam about 1". Mark lower point of opening for sleeve on side seam about 7"-9" below shoulder. Add ½" seam allowance to shoulder and side edges.

3. To make front, draw a rectangle the desired length of jacket by one quarter of the chest measurement including ease. Using back pattern as a guide mark edge of neckline, slope of shoulders and opening for sleeve. Draw curve of front neckline using girl's neck or other garment as guide. Add ½" to center front edge. Add ½" seam allowance to neck, shoulder and side edges.

4. Measure desired length of sleeves. Measure armhole area on jacket front and back. Draw a rectangle using these measurements. Measure wrist or sleeve width on jacket and determine desired width of lower edge of sleeve. Mark this width on rectangle and taper side edges of sleeves. Add ½" seam allowance on sides and upper edge.

Cutting

1. Cut 1 back, 2 fronts and 2 sleeves from lining fabric and quilt batting. Baste quilt batting to wrong side of fabric pieces ⅜" from edges. Baste pieces of jacket together and try on. Make any adjustments to patterns at this point. Remove basted seams of jacket.

2. To make block for jacket back, follow directions on page 12. Cut all cat's body, face and tail pieces from orange dot fabric. Cut background pieces from lime green. Trace nose onto fusible webbing and cut from yellow. Omit border pieces. Cut two 8½" x 1½" borders and two 10½" x 1½" borders.

3. To make blocks for jacket front, cut cat's face and neck pieces from orange dot fabric. Cut background pieces from turquoise. Cut nose from yellow. Do not cut tail section yet.

4. Reverse face and neck pieces and cut from yellow dot fabric. Cut background pieces from purple. Cut nose from bright pink.

5. Cut one 4½" square of lime green and one 4½" square of purple. Extend tail pattern 1¼" on lower edge (template found on page 33). Make an orange dot appliqué tail piece using this pattern. Reverse pattern and cut a yellow dot appliqué tail.

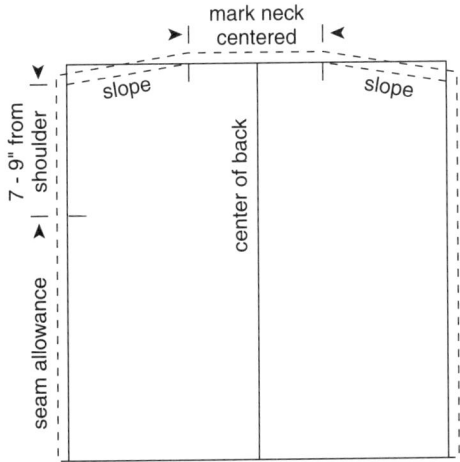

6. From each purple and turquoise, cut two 5½" x 1" border piece and two 6½" x 1" border pieces. From each turquoise and lime green, cut two 5½" x 1½" pocket borders and two 7½" x 1½" pocket borders. Cut a 5" square pocket from each turquoise and lime green. Cut two 5" squares from quilt batting.

7. Cut a few 5½" squares of dotted and print fabrics. Cut a 5½" square of purple and lime green.

8. Cut 3¼" wide bias strips to make a binding to go around neck, center front and lower edge of jacket. Cut two bias strips to bind lower edge of sleeve. Cut a 1" wide bias strip 18" long to make button loops.

Directions

1. For back make center of cat block following directions on pages 12-13. Fuse nose in place and zigzag stitch around it. Stitch 8½" purple block borders to top and bottom edges of block. Stitch 10½" borders to side edges.

2. Place block on jacket back with quilt batting side up matching vertical centers. Arrange 5½" patchwork squares around sides and lower edges of cat block alternating colors and prints.

3. Stitch blocks together along sides in pairs. Place these pieces along side edges of block with right sides together matching edges. Stitch ¼" from edge of patchwork. Fold fabric over seam to cover quilt batting. Trim fabric even with edge of batting and lining.

4. Cut a piece of one of the cat prints to fit area above cat block. Place along top edge of block with right sides together matching edges. Stitch ¼" from edge of patchwork. Fold fabric over seam to cover quilt batting. Trim fabric even with edge of batting and lining.

5. Stitch four fabric squares below block together. Place along lower edge of block with right sides together matching edges. Stitch ¼" from edge of patchwork. Fold fabric over seam to cover quilt batting. Trim fabric even with edge of batting and lining.

6. Cut a strip of striped fabric to cover area below patchwork squares, if needed. Stitch to jacket in same manner.

7. Make cat face squares following steps 1-3, pages 12-13. Stitch purple borders to square with orange face and lime pocket borders to square with yellow face.

8. Appliqué yellow tail to purple 4½" solid square and the orange tail to the lime square, following step 4 on page 13. Add turquoise borders to the orange tail square and turquoise pocket borders to the yellow tail square.

9. Stitch a 5½" print square to lower edge of each small orange cat block. Stitch 4" turquoise square to lower edge of strip with face. Stitch 4" lime square to lower edge of strip with tail. Place these pieces centered on the fronts.

10. Cut a 10½" long piece of one of the cat prints to fit area on sides of strips. Stitch a patchwork square to lower edge of each piece. Place along side edge of center strips with right sides together matching edges and seams. Stitch ¼" from edge of patchwork. Fold fabric over seam to cover quilt batting. Trim fabric even with edge of batting and lining.

11. Cut a piece of another print to cover area at top of fronts. Place along top edge of block with right sides together matching edges. Stitch ¼" from edge of patchwork. Fold fabric over seam to cover quilt batting. Trim fabric even with edge of batting and lining.

12. Cut a strip of striped fabric to cover area below patchwork, if needed. Stitch to jacket in same manner.

13. For pockets, baste quilt batting to remaining patchwork squares. Right sides together, stitch matching solid squares to pockets using ½" seam allowance and leaving an opening for turning at lower edge. Trim seam allowance. Turn right side out. Slipstitch edges of opening together.

14. For sleeves, stitch three patchwork squares together. Place along lower edge of sleeve. Cut a piece of striped fabric to cover top area of sleeve

5. Quilt along seams of patchwork. Place along top edge of patchwork strip with right sides together matching edges. Stitch ¼" from edge of patchwork. Fold fabric over seam to cover quilt batting. Trim fabric even with edge of batting and lining.

16. Baste edges of each jacket piece together ⅜" from raw edges. Quilt along edges of patchwork.

Assembling

Stitch all seams right sides together using ½" seam allowance. Lightly press seams open. Zigzag stitch seam allowances.

1. Sew pockets over solid patches on fronts.

2. Stitch fronts to back along shoulder edges.

3. Stitch sleeves to side edge of front and back.

4. Matching fronts to backs stitch underarm and side seams.

5. Fold button loop strip in half lengthwise with right sides together. Stitch ¼" from fold. Trim seam allowance to ⅛". Turn right side out using a small pin or bodkin. To determine length of each loop, measure amount needed to go around button plus ½" seam allowance at each end. On lining side of right front, position 6 loops evenly spaced along center front as shown in diagram. Baste in place.

6. Following directions on page 6, bind neck, front and lower edge of jacket. Bind lower edge of sleeves.

7. Sew buttons to left front of jacket. Sew buttons to cat's faces for eyes. Embroider whiskers in black using long straight stitches.

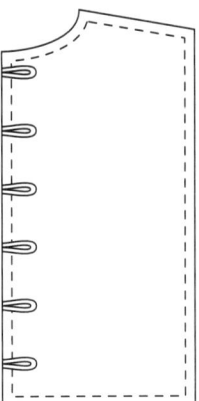

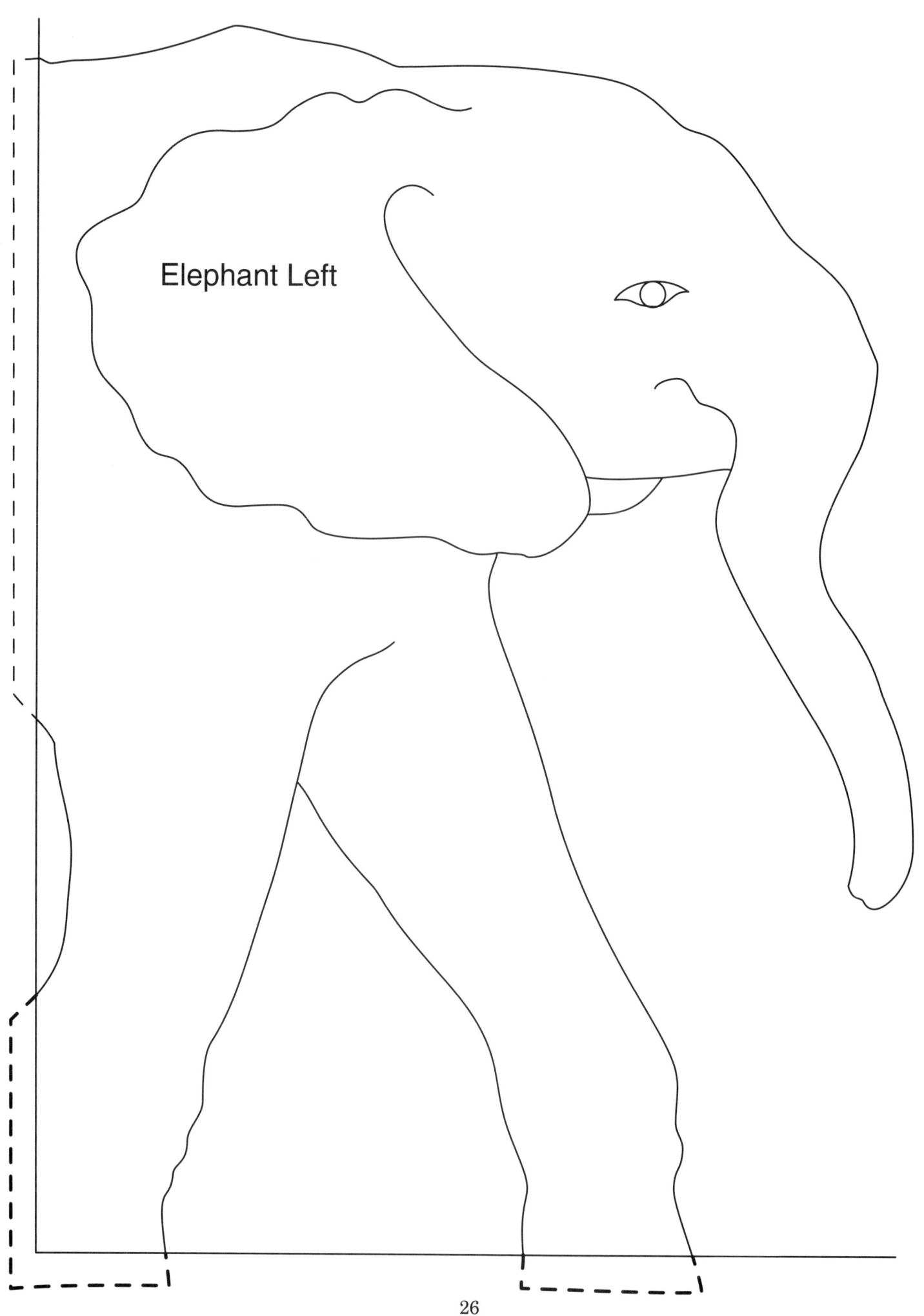

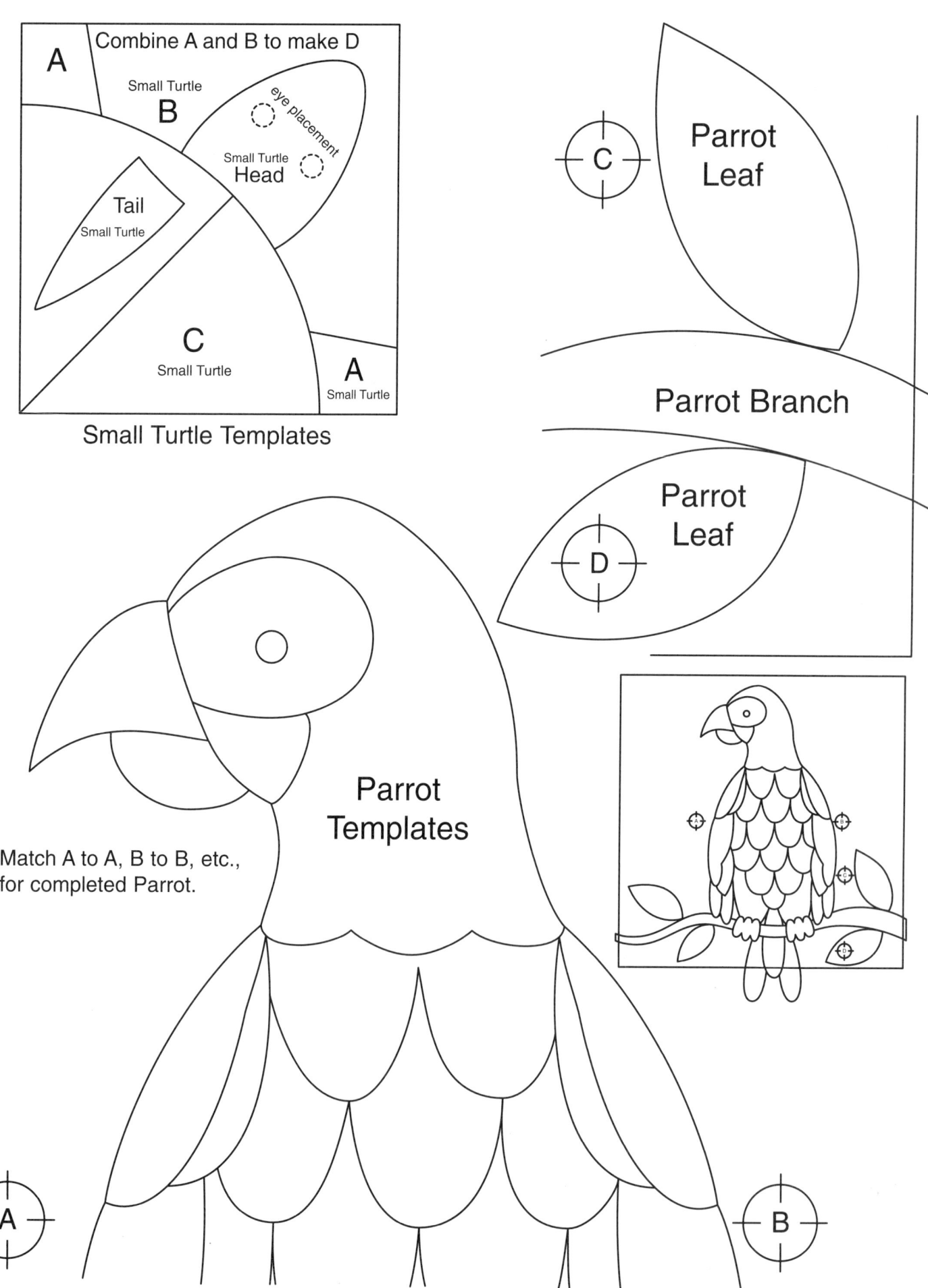

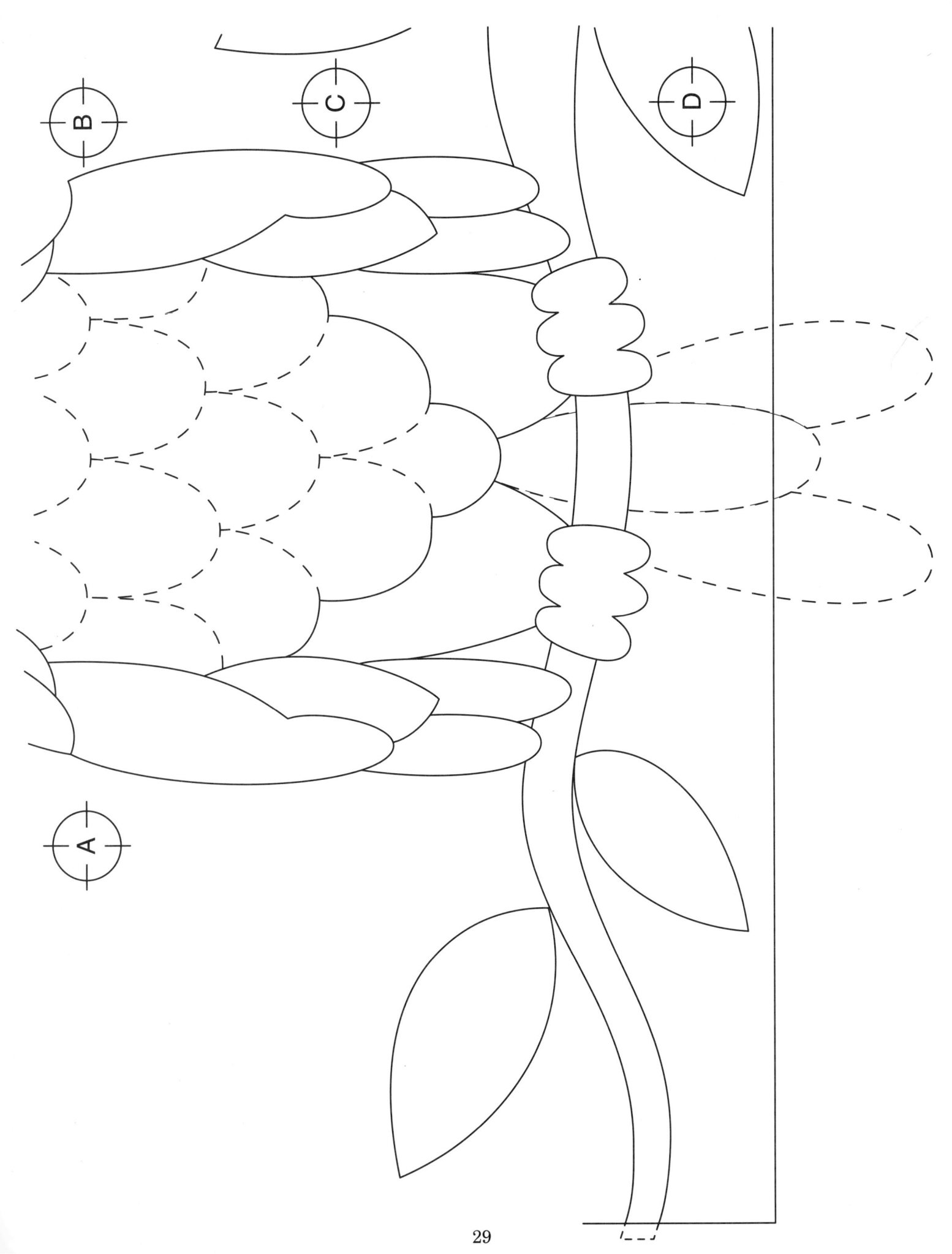

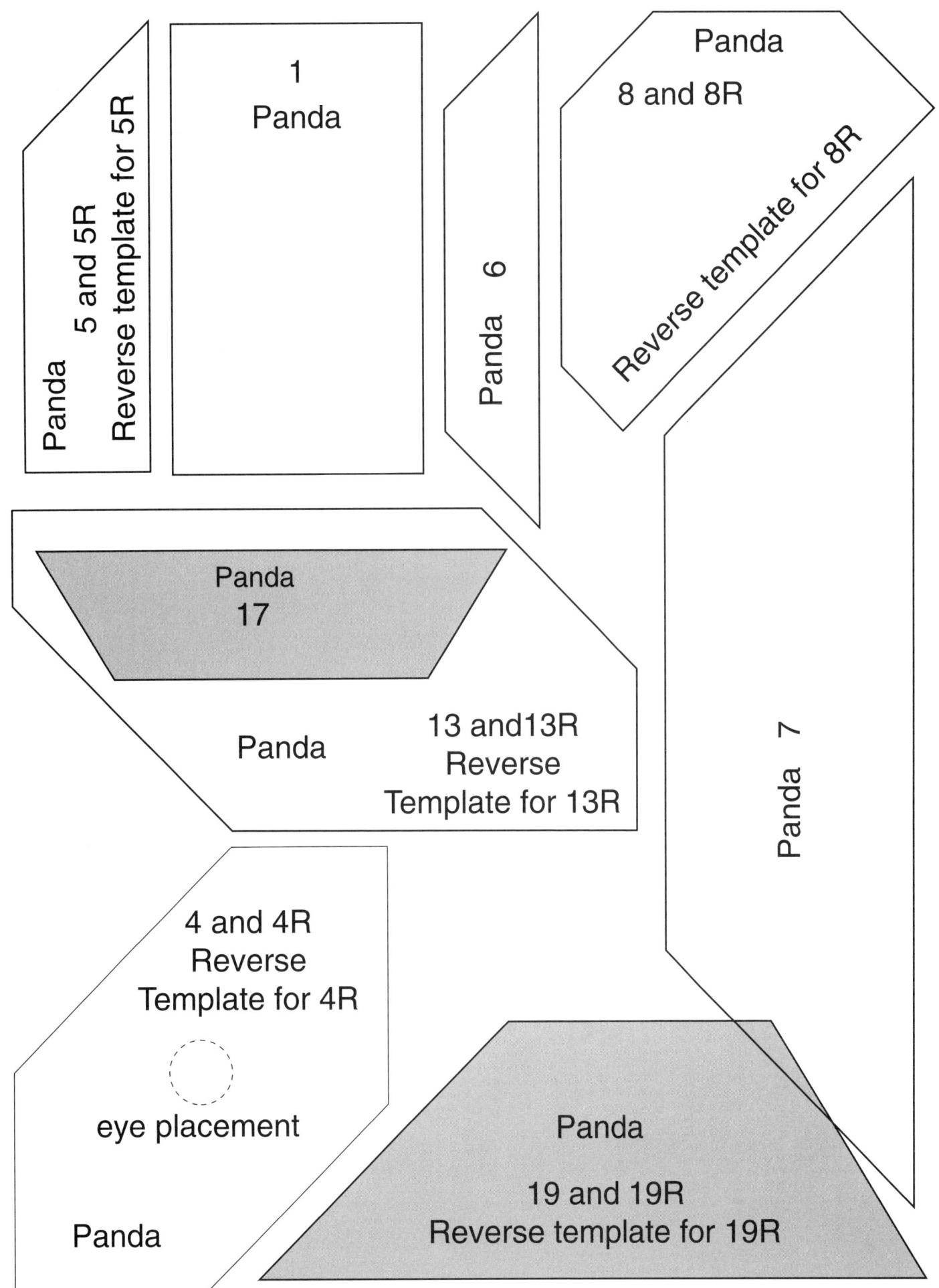

Fish
E
D
Fish
Fish
C
Fish
B
Fish
C
Fish
B
Fish
A
F
(For
Pillow)
Fish
D
C
Fish
C
Fish
Fish
A
G
(For Pillow)

11
Panda
Panda
20
3
Panda
Panda
18
9
Panda
10
Panda
Panda
12
Panda
14
Panda
2

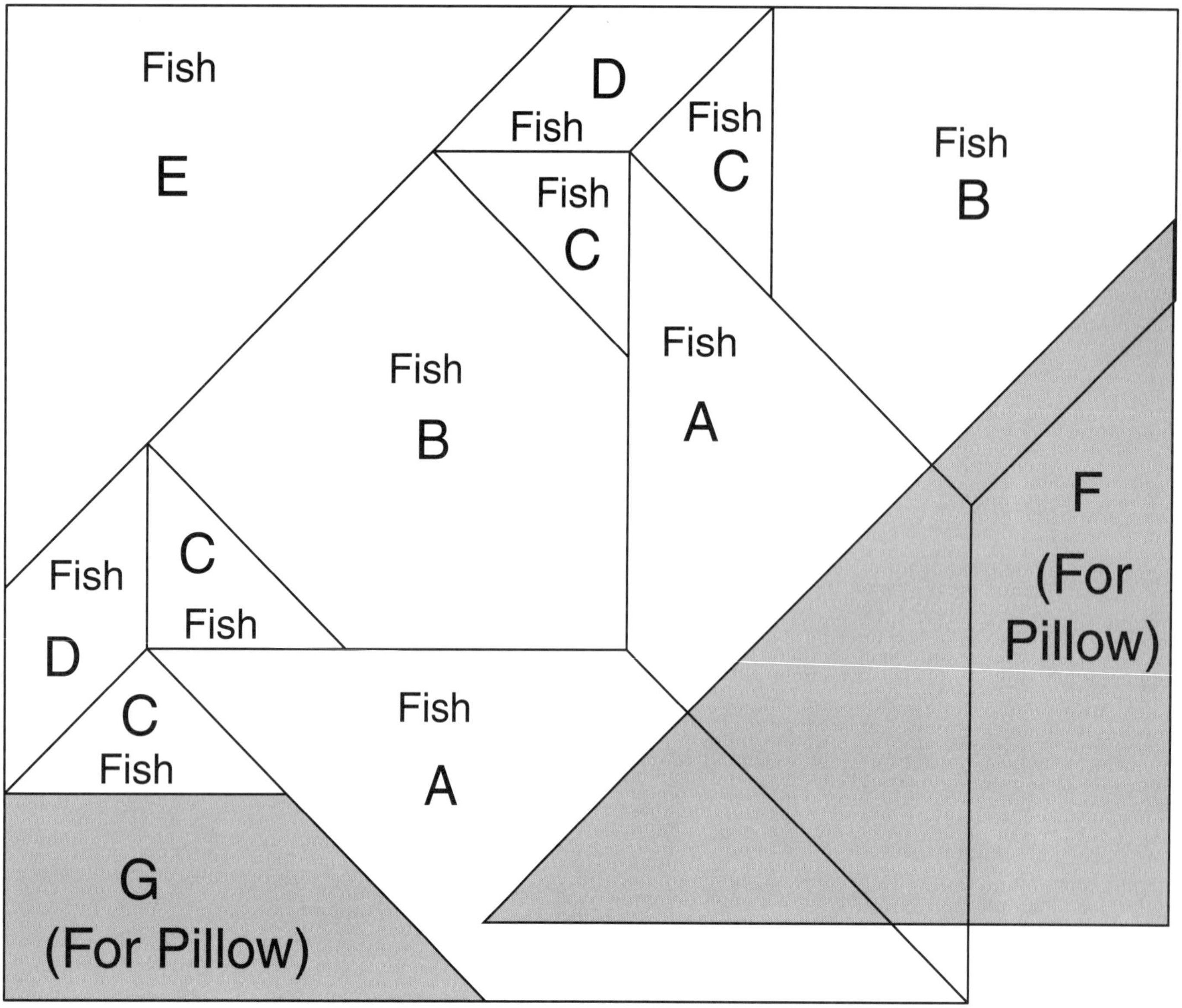

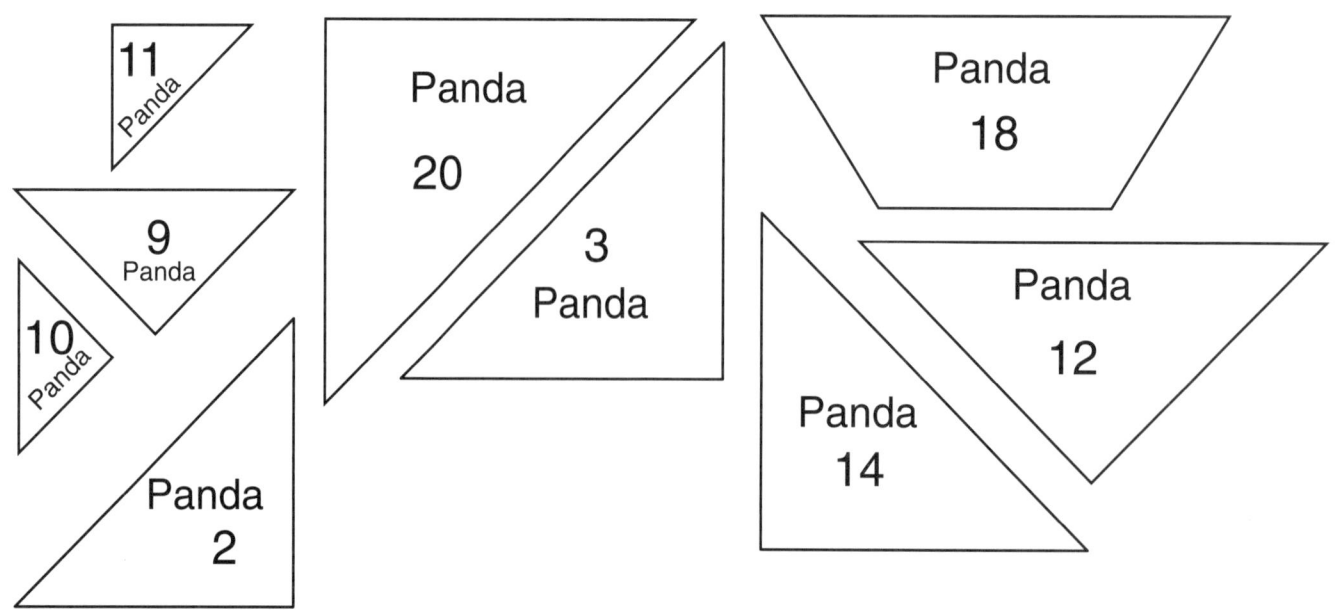

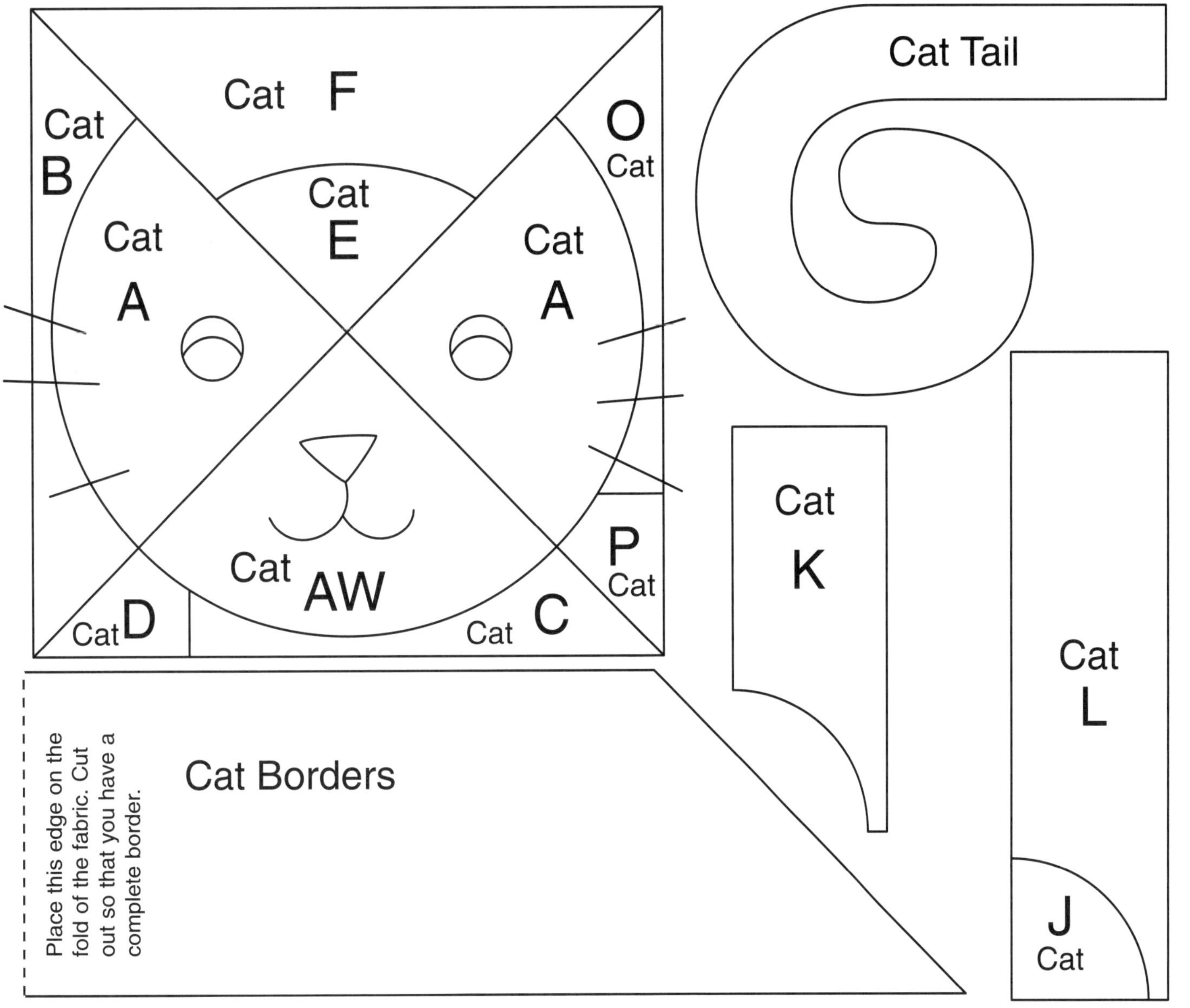

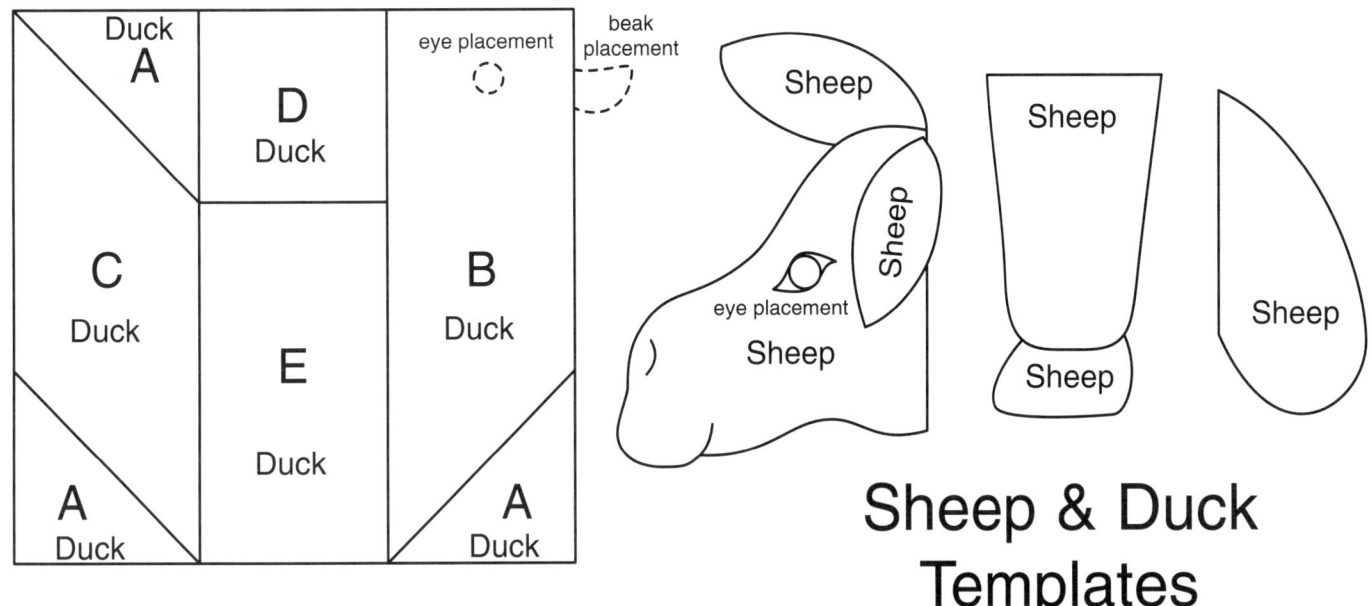

Sheep & Duck Templates

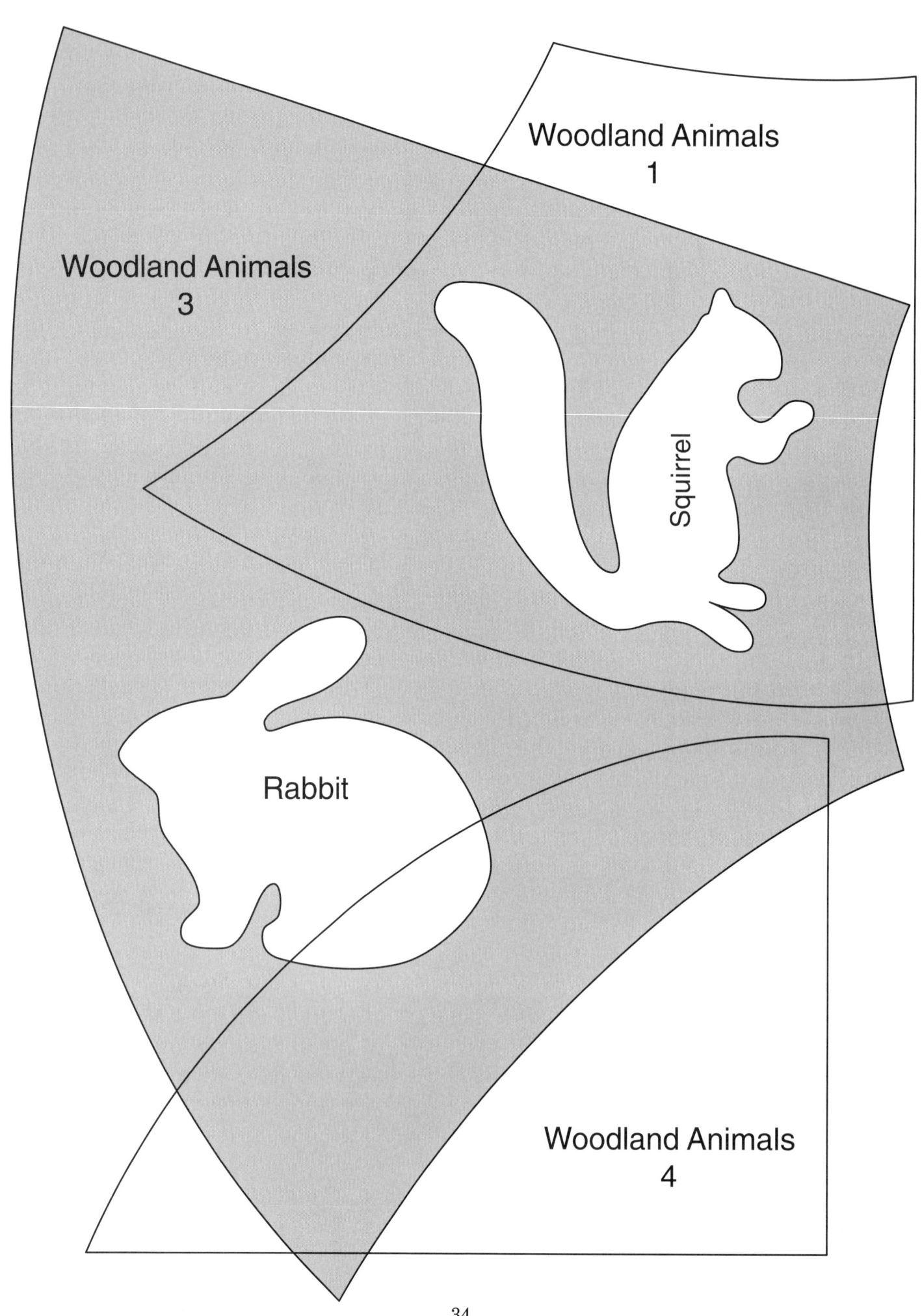

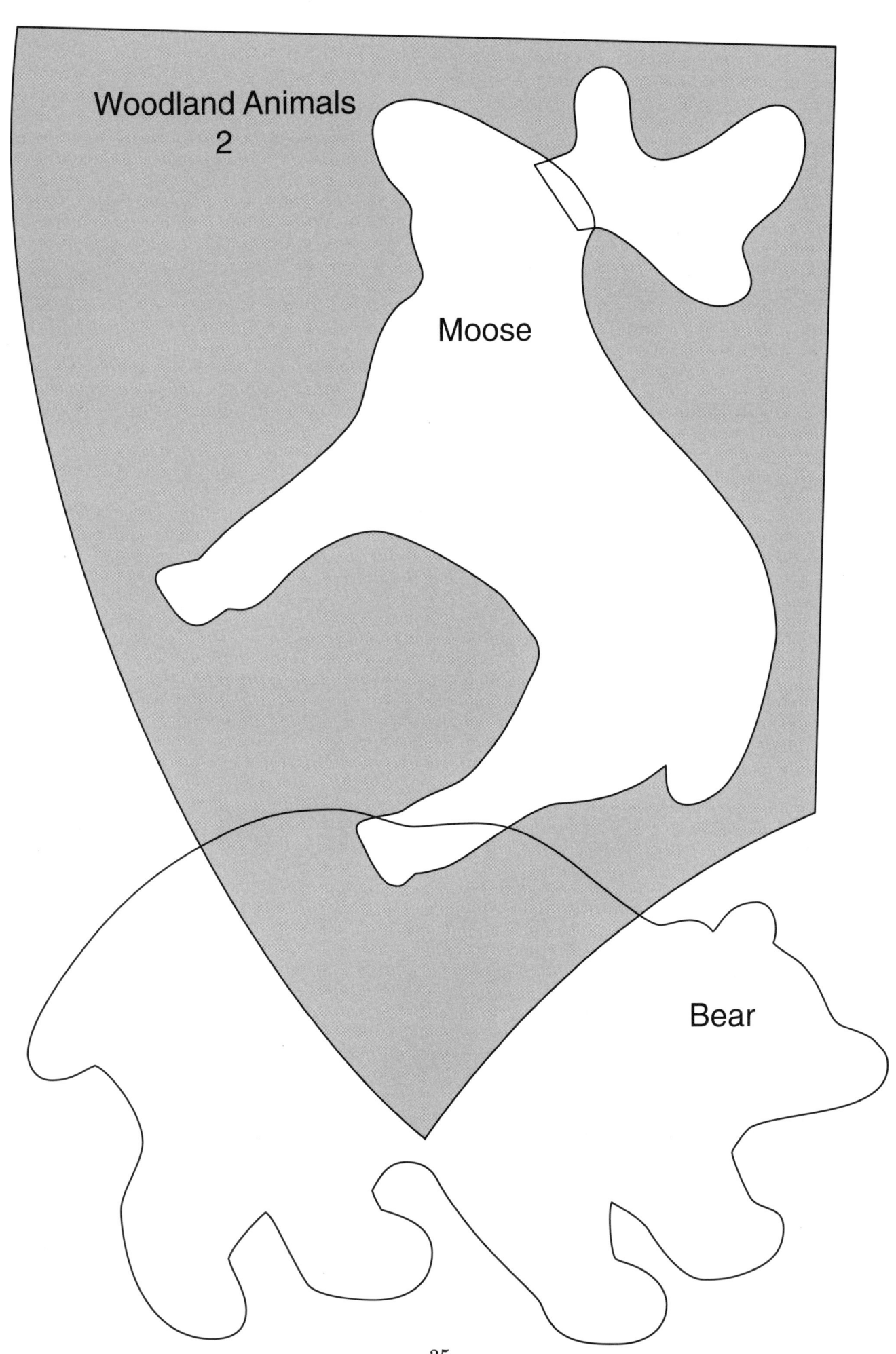

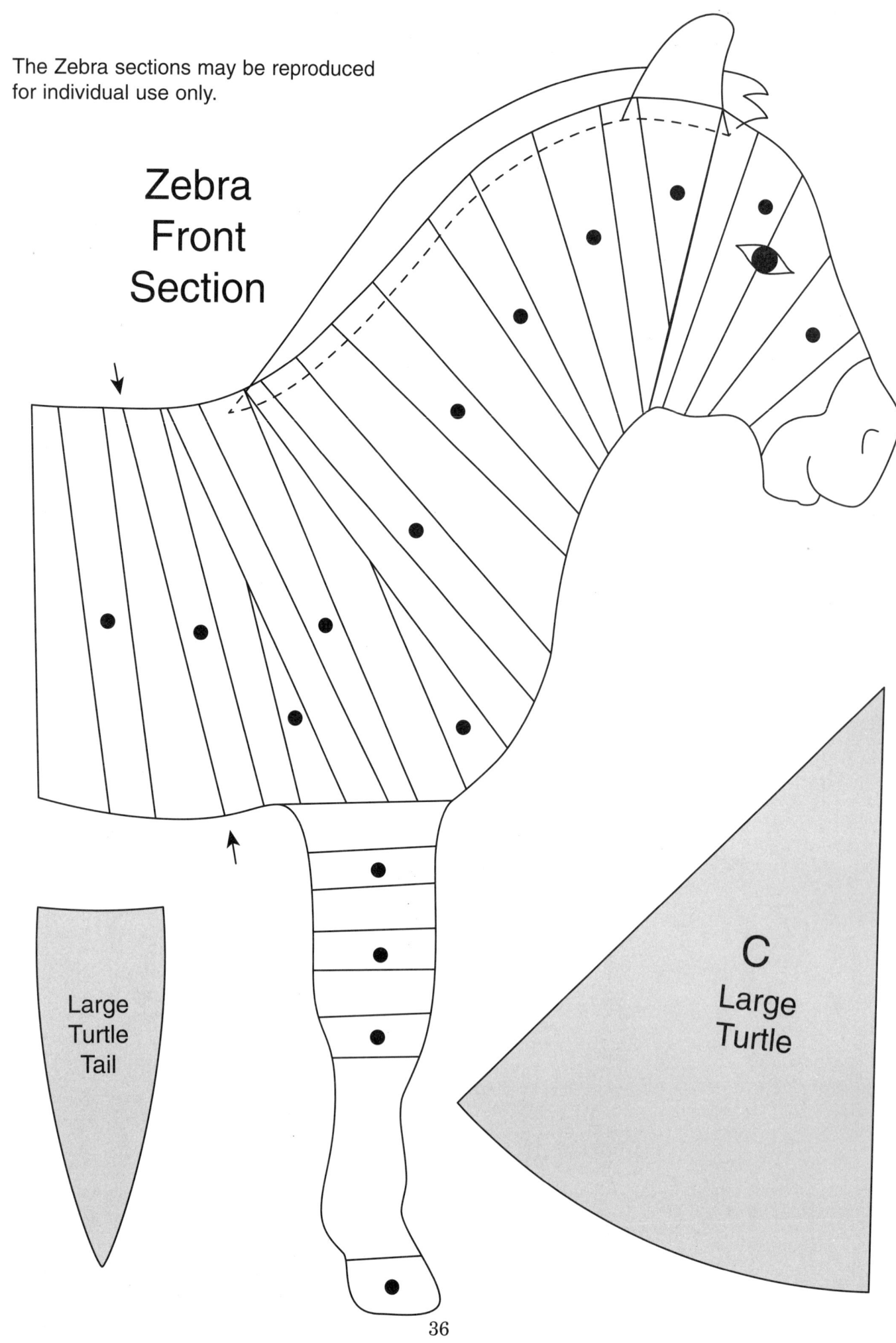

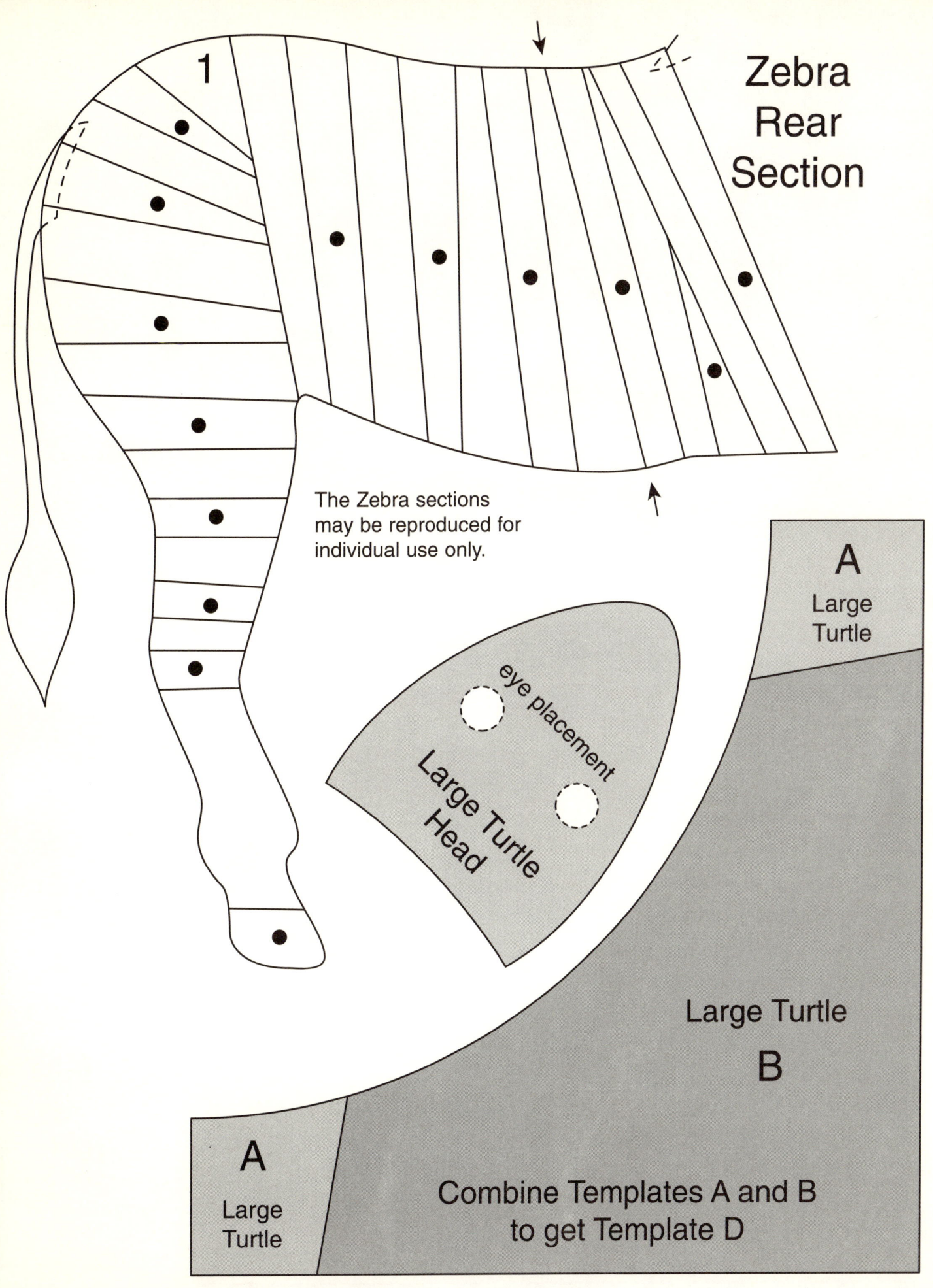

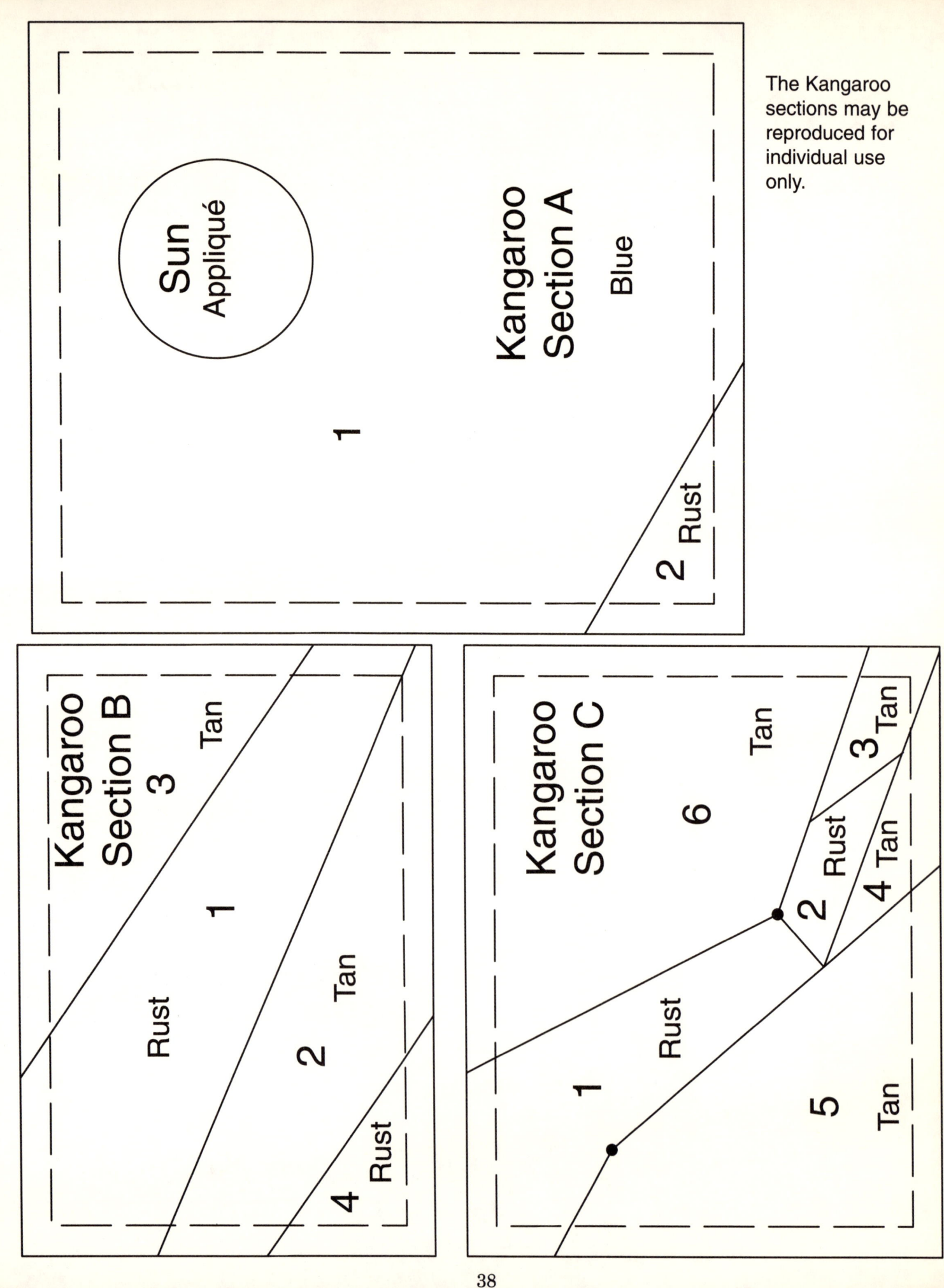

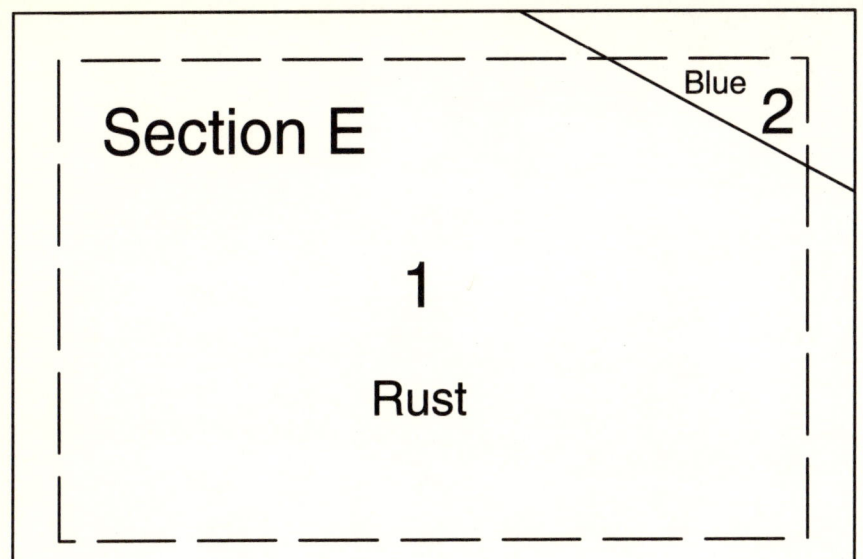
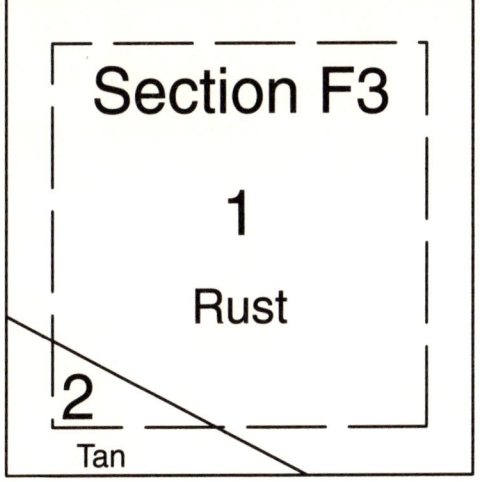
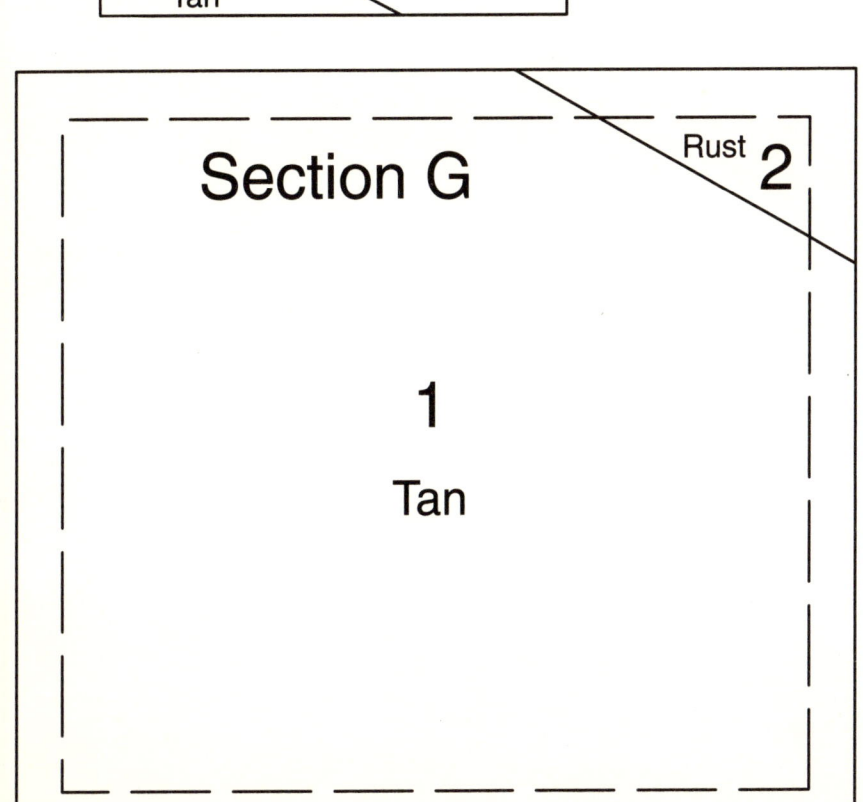
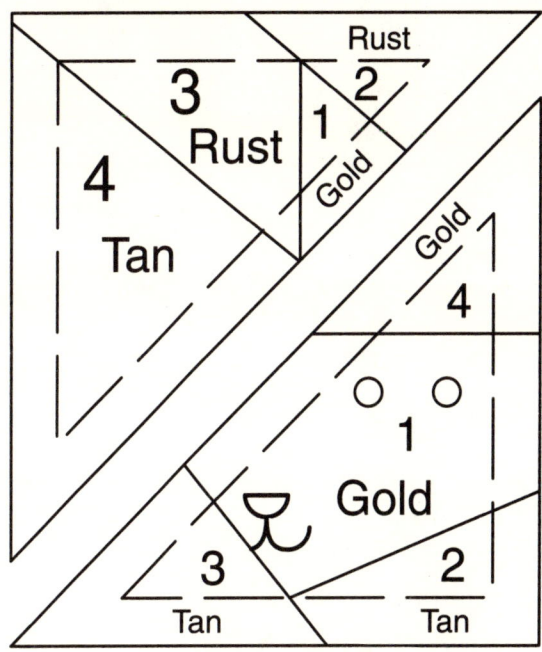
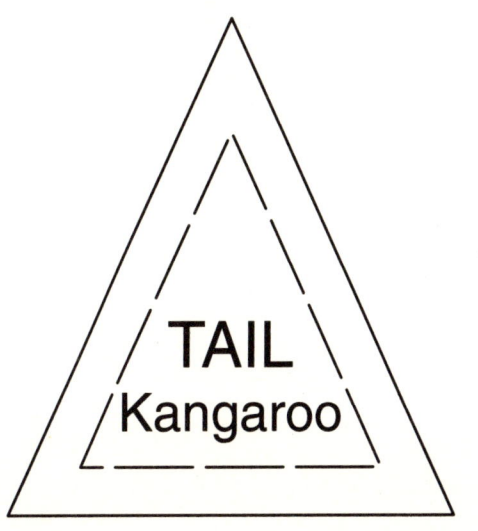

The Kangaroo sections may be reproduced for individual use only.

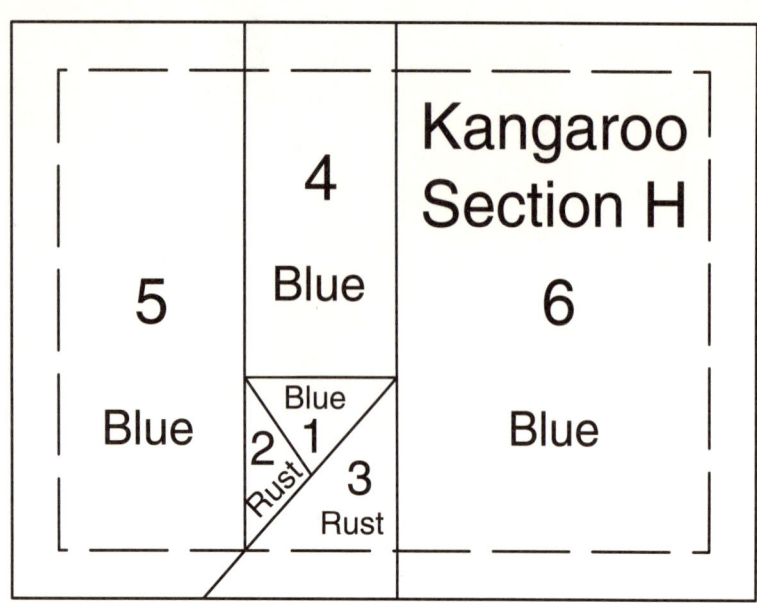

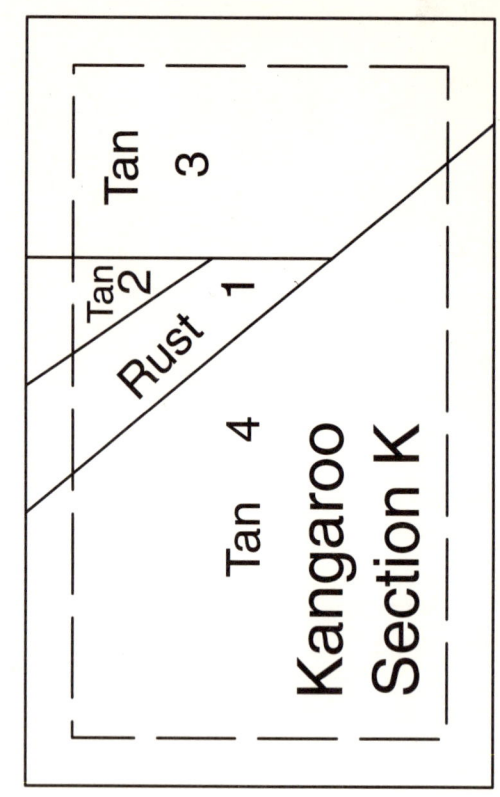

The Kangaroo sections may be reproduced for individual use only.

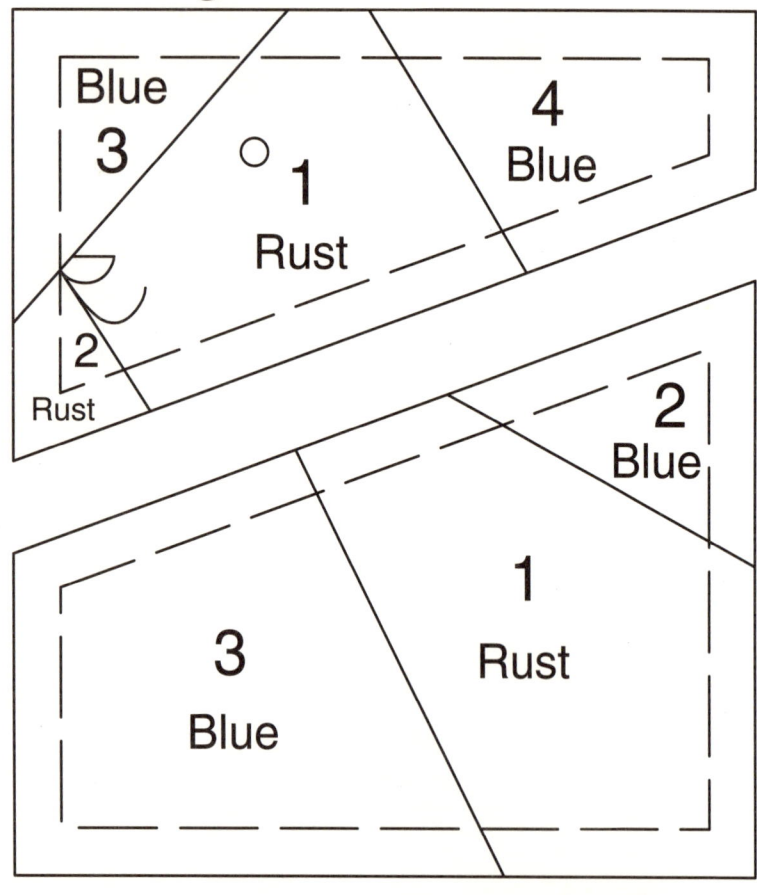

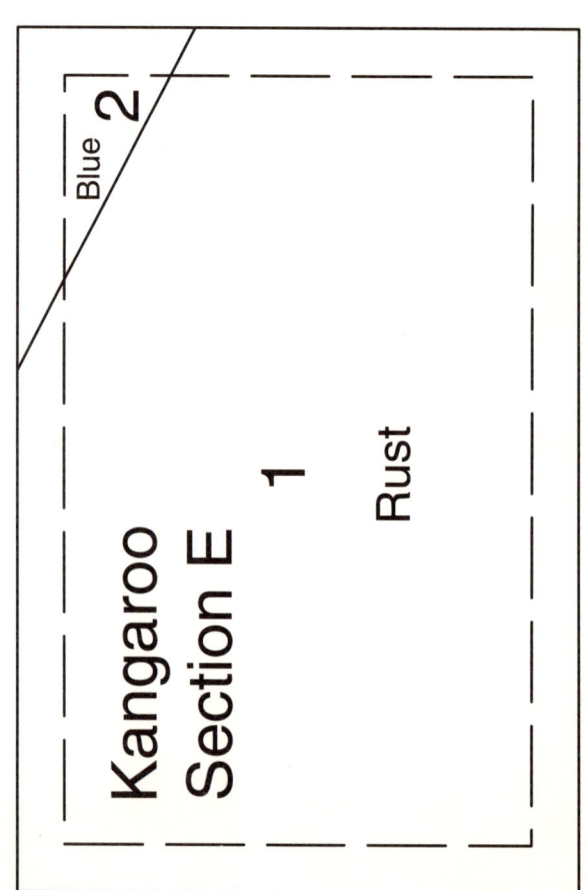